Hearing for John

Defying the
challenges of hearing loss

by

John Marshall Mills

North Somerset Library Service	
1 9 2508625 8	
Askews	22-Nov-2007
305.908	£12.49

AuthorHouse™
1663 Liberty Drive, Suite 200
Bloomington, IN 47403
www.authorhouse.com
Phone: 1-800-839-8640

AuthorHouse™ UK Ltd.
500 Avebury Boulevard
Central Milton Keynes, MK9 2BE
www.authorhouse.co.uk
Phone: 08001974150

© 2006 John Marshall Mills. All rights reserved.

*No part of this book may be reproduced, stored in
a retrieval system, or transmitted by any means
without the written permission of the author.*

First published by AuthorHouse 12/18/2006

ISBN: 978-1-4259-8600-1 (sc)

Library of Congress Control Number: 2006911026

Printed in the United States of America
Bloomington, Indiana

This book is printed on acid-free paper.

To the many people whose kindness and patience
have helped me to connect over the years,
my sincere thanks.

It's harder to find words rich enough
to express my feelings about the tireless support that
I have received from my beloved family.
I can only say, with all my heart,
thank you
Tricia,
Amanda and Tom,
Guy and Amanda,
and
Samantha.

In addition, special thanks

to Michael Guy and other hearing
professionals for their thoughts;

to The British Academy of Audiology, The British
Society of Audiology, The British Society of Hearing
Aid Audiologists, The Hearing Aid Council, The
Eye Care Trust, PC Werth Ltd., Lee Fletcher,
and Jonathan Parsons for questions answered;

to Soraya Berry for her constructive
advice and editing;
and
to the team at authorHouse for
putting this work into print.

Contents

	Introduction	1
	Our Fighting Spirit	4
	A Few Important Pointers	9
John	Is it my imagination?	15
Tricia	So much taken for granted	16
John	Hard to be honest with myself	18
Tricia	Has he really not heard me?	22
John	What my friends won't tell me	24
Samantha	Never seems to bother him somehow	30
John	I will always have choices	33
Amanda	He will never give up	36
John	Sounds make sense of things	38
Tricia	A little bit of history	43
John	Sooner or later I had to...	45
Professional	Breaking the ice	49
John	My big learning curve	51
Tricia	Our noisy world	58
John	Devils in the decodes	60
Professional	It's all about trust	66
John	Great expectations	68
Professional	Starting gently	73
John	How is it for me?	74
Professional	Loud or quiet, it's always there	79
John	My problem, your problem	80
Professional	New hearing, new learning	84
John	'Flavours' of hearing are subtle: discuss	87
Tricia	Some choice!!	96
John	Ignorance or indifference?	98
Tricia	Badges of pride?	102

John	Brainpower on my side	105
Tricia	Getting on his good side	110
John	Most valuable of my valuables	112
Tricia	Moments that make you smile	121
John	Keywords to open my ears	123
Tricia	Telephones	127
John	Life goes on, we go with it	131
Tricia	Shades of difference	135
John	Some do's and don'ts	137
Tricia	Feedback	145
John	How to stay connected	147
Tricia	Lost in transmission	150
John	Never the same twice?	151
Tricia	Games of care	155
John	Accepting reality	158
Tricia	Tale of the unexpected	163
John	Staying positive	164
Tricia	How to get out?	167
John	Hiss and friends	168
Tricia	Progress of a sort?	171
John	Looking forward	173
John	Personal background	178
	Useful Contacts	180

Introduction

'You won't care until it happens to you' is true of many of life's hazards but it has a special resonance with hearing loss because of the way it impacts on our ability to connect, impedes the flow of our thoughts, strikes at the core of who we are and dictates our quality of life. For many of us deafness has an image that is far from uplifting – although, thankfully, this is changing.

So let me highlight one of the most important thoughts that I believe all of us who have hearing loss should embrace.

Hiding our difficulty casts a shadow on our life. Sharing it lets in the sun.

This book is not intended to be a technical handbook or a guide to solutions for hearing loss. That kind of authoritative support is readily available from far better-qualified sources prominent among them RNID, Hearing Concern and Deafness Research UK. These energetically proactive charities for people who are deaf and hard of hearing are being increasingly successful in changing attitudes and awareness and in stimulating positive practical help. (See Useful Contacts later.)

Instead, three main reasons that have prompted me to attempt these pages:

1. To give a wholly personal insider view of partial and progressive deafness in the hope that, if you also have this problem, sharing my experiences may help you with your own positive way forward.

2. To sound the alert that many of you, not yet affected, may face hearing loss either personally or through someone close to you. The problem is growing and there is no room for complacency.
3. To highlight ignorance and indifference about deafness, and the impact this has on those of us who are directly involved.

If you are 'one of us' take heart. Many things are getting better. You are a member of a large and regrettably fast-growing community. An estimated nine million of us in the United Kingdom (one in seven of the whole population) are known to have hearing loss, and other estimates suggest that there are a further four million with hearing problems that have yet to be officially acknowledged. These figures do not include our families, friends and working colleagues who are regularly involved with the consequences of hearing problems through their contacts with us.

If someone in your family has hearing loss, or if you are in regular contact with anyone who is hard of hearing, what you read here should help you to understand some of the difficulties and thoughts that they experience, and this may enable you to offer support that is perceptive and therefore constructive, as well as being sympathetic. You may also get some insight into the 'private' world that hearing loss prompts us to develop for ourselves.

If you are a hearing professional, most if not all of these jottings will be familiar and you would no doubt be able to fill many more pages with interesting anecdotes and helpful advice. However maybe – just maybe – you will find the occasional thought here that will prompt you to view a particular topic from a different angle. I hope you will.

While you read what follows, be clear that your experiences and your point of view are unlikely to be exactly the same as the ones that I and other contributors describe. We each have our own path and our own choices to make in finding solutions.

For more than thirty years my family and I have had to handle a steady decline in my hearing. In explaining how this has affected them personally my wife Tricia, and my daughters Amanda and Samantha have contributed their own perspectives. They know how much I value their input and support. I am also indebted to hearing aid audiologists who have described their experiences and thinking which add an important professional point of view.

Frustrations there have been but also many moments of refreshing insight and not a little humour, all of which help to keep me optimistic about the future.

Our Fighting Spirit

There are a number of attitudes that our hearing loss can generate in others:

>Pity it, patronise it.
>Use it as an excuse to ignore us.
>Take advantage of our discomfort.
>or
>Admire our attitude.
>Do everything possible to provide active support.
>Take note of all that is involved against the day when they too may suffer from it, which is increasingly likely in our noisy world.

Hearing loss cannot be concealed. Why should it be? If we declare it, share it, wear it as a badge that we are not ashamed of, inviting the world to accept us as we are, then we give others the chance, even the incentive, to find ways of helping us to adapt to their 'normality'. If we are completely open we show that we are not afraid and we automatically make it difficult for others to raise it as an issue.

When they see that we are being strong, fearless about our personal circumstances; when we demonstrate how determined we are to overcome any disadvantages that we are experiencing; and whenever we show that we have the strength to fight the negative attitudes that hearing difficulties so often generate we give them the encouragement to find ways to help us.

This fighting spirit not only provides good reason for them to respect us, it also does wonders for our own self-respect. We owe this much to ourselves and also to everyone who offers us support. Every gesture of care towards our difficulties deserves an equally caring response from us, a vitally important part of building bridges. Above all, this should eliminate any temptation to make comparisons in which we feel second best.

One of the most valuable keys in dealing with hearing loss is discovering how to be happy with ourselves. Hearing is only one of our senses, only one part of us. It is surely wrong to allow it to dominate us. Of course we can't ignore the problems it causes but we can be more aware of our own positive values. Our track record, interests and skills all have a special personal dimension. We can and should be proactive in recognising how many strengths we have.

We have good reason to be optimistic about the future. Awareness and support for those of us who are deaf and hard of hearing are growing significantly thanks in no small part to the energetic activities of the hearing charities and a steadily expanding army of caring professionals and volunteers. The pace of innovations and invention is getting faster. For the moment, however, we have to recognise that many of the options hearing professionals can offer have limits. This means that we have to be prepared to accept compromises and find our own ways of handling problems that cannot be corrected perfectly. However if our attitude is confident and encourages us to feel positive about the advice and solutions we are being offered, we will get the best out of them, sometimes with startling results.

We *can* get used to hearing loss and work out how we fit into the different world it creates. We do this in the same way as we do with everything else – trial and error. This is where we can benefit from the infinite flexibility of the brain. It really has no limits except those we impose out of our lack of confidence. A small child learning how to eat or toddle shows how much we can achieve. The child tries, and tries again until eventually the brain lets it arrive at a way of achieving its goal. We can do the same in working out a different approach to hearing and in discovering our own special ways to make up for any deficiency.

Attitude is something we can change by making sure that we stay in charge of our thoughts. How we feel and how we live depend entirely on how we think. And although we may believe that some of our instincts are fixed, there is no thought we have that we cannot change. This is critically important in the way we think about loss of hearing. We can completely transform its effect on the way we live by altering the way we think about it. We can constructively create an attitude that makes it easier for us to handle any confusion and frustration that we feel. We can change our negative thoughts to positive and, when we do, we immediately have an impact on the physical performance of our hearing.

Negative to positive – but how? The secret is simple. We do it by creating our own benchmarks, accepting our own limits and living within them without worrying that we are not exactly keeping time with other 'normalities'. In setting our goals we make sure they are modest steps to begin with, realistically possible for us. Every target that we achieve, no matter how small, is a boost for our self-respect. When we manage it we reward ourselves with a pat on the back. Each one is a building block in the new approach we have to our hearing and to the way we live. We have our own rules. And we need to see how well we can get everyone else to help us make them work. Our main aim must be to feel comfortable with ourselves.

How we achieve this will always be very personal. It is tempting for me to suggest a list of helpful hints but there will always be omissions and suggestions that do not suit your unique situation. It is here that hearing professionals can provide invaluable support. A hearing therapist who learns about your very individual needs will have the experience and sensitivity to propose ideas that will suit you and make a positive difference.

There is one crucially important point to be absolutely clear about: we don't have to accept that our difficulty is a burden we must shoulder alone. There is no end to the support we can receive when we teach ourselves to notice the goodwill that is available to us. Yet, we are also free to identify our own horizons. We need never give up on ourselves even if we are told nothing more can be done (as has twice happened to me). There is always someone new for us to consult, something new to try and with every new choice there is always the possibility of an unexpectedly rewarding solution. Hearing loss is never typical. It is personal. And, with its never-ending flexibility and adaptability, our brain gives us the perfect secret weapon to find our own solutions and successes.

Hearing for John

We *can* overcome any feeling of obligation or weakness by becoming much more aware of how independent we can be. We are normal in our own way even if this is different from the normality which large numbers of people accept. With our new ways of hearing we are new individuals with our own new take on the world. We have our own very unique point of view. This is something that we must teach ourselves to value. Being different, being special is what being individual is all about. We can enjoy the feeling of personal power that it gives us in playing the games of life.

Hearing loss can be like a cold rainy day. We can hide indoors, or we can put on appropriate clothes and get on with our life. No day is so wet and cold that we have to give up. The choice will always be ours.

A Few Important Pointers

In any story centred around hearing loss there are a number of general explanations that any newcomer will find helpful. Do bear in mind this is not a complete list; simply some headlines based on my own experiences.

How can I know if I am deaf and need help?

If you don't think your hearing is as good as it was, your first call has to be to your doctor. There can be any number of reasons for your symptoms – many of them not caused by actual deafness. For example, a blockage caused by ear wax can usually be easily removed, but *only* trust a doctor or qualified nurse. So don't feel alarmed. Let your GP put your mind at rest one way or another.

Will I need a hearing specialist?

If your GP thinks your hearing needs to be looked at further you may be referred to an ENT (ear, nose and throat) consultant/specialist or, in some cases, to an audiologist. It was my ENT specialist who recommended that I should have a hearing aid.

What is an audiologist?

An audiologist studies and treats hearing and balance problems. A qualified audiologist will have made a close study of the ear and its associated problems during their degree course. Assessing your ears, prescribing, fitting and adjusting the most appropriate make and type of hearing aid that will work best with your hearing loss, and then offering expert after-care, are usual ingredients in the audiology service. Some independent companies that dispense hearing aids also offer the services of an audiologist.

What about hearing aid dispensers?

Registered hearing aid dispensers are also qualified to prescribe and fit hearing aids. Hearing aid dispensers (also called hearing aid audiologists) use similar skills as audiologists in prescribing and fitting hearing aids and then adjusting them to suit the personal hearing profile of the patient. The skill of both the dispenser and the audiologist in working with the extremely advanced technology of the latest digital hearing aids can make a crucial difference to the quality of your hearing. Note that some hearing professionals prefer to call us clients.

Hearing tests

Before any decision can be taken about prescribing a hearing aid, you will be given a hearing test. I have lost count of the times I have been tested and have always found it a simple, painless stress-free procedure. The aim of the basic test is to discover how well you can hear a range of sound frequencies from the lowest sounds to the highest, and then to plot the results on an audiogram graph.

Hearing aids?

Hearing aids are described as either **analogue** or **digital**. An analogue aid takes in sound waves and amplifies the frequencies directly. A digital aid has a tiny computer which processes sounds. It can be programmed to adjust to your specific hearing loss.

If you get a hearing aid privately it's likely you will be buying digital.

The NHS can now offer the majority of people digital aids following a programme to modernise its hearing aid service.

Digital hearing aids have become progressively smaller and more discreet to the point where some are almost invisible. But remember, the best digital hearing aid for you may not be invisible or tiny! Cosmetic and aesthetic advantages will never be the most important consideration. We need enough power to give the right kind of help for our hearing loss. Competition between the leading makers of hearing aids is fierce. Our safeguard should be the experience and expertise of audiologists and dispensers in making an objective judgement about which make and model will be best for us. Outside the NHS, cost can be a big consideration, especially where there is a choice between different versions and extras offered with the same make. Whichever one they recommend, audiologists and hearing aid dispensers will usually try to ensure that we don't have unrealistic expectations about possible improvements in our hearing.

If you do decide to go down the private route, try to get as much information as possible from organisations such as the British Academy of Audiology or from the hearing charities' websites and helplines. There are some useful contact details at the end of the book.

Just one word of warning. An off-the-shelf aid, bought without professional advice from a doctor or audiologist, may not give you all the benefits you need including an adequate allowance for follow-up fine tuning and more general after-care.

Information and support

The world of deafness is in a state of constant change. Not only are there new technologies and treatments coming onto the market but public awareness and attitudes are becoming more positive and helpful. A lot of credit for this must go to the work of the UK charities which have not only been very active in lobbying and promoting positive support for people with hearing loss but are also extremely helpful in providing advice and information. Knowing from personal experience how much important detail is available from their publications and websites, I can only urge that you seriously consider offering these charities your support, and avail yourself of their many services.

As an example of what is on offer I quote from the first page of RNID's excellent booklet *'the essential guide'* (volume 2):

- *There are an estimated nine million deaf and hard of hearing people in the UK.*
- *Tinnitus affects 4.7 million adults.*
- *There are an estimated 2,474,000 deaf and hard of hearing people aged 16 to 60.*
- *More than 70% of people over 70 will have some kind of hearing loss.*

An easy-to-read mine of information, this RNID guide covers hearing aids, lipreading, British Sign Language, tinnitus, cochlear implants, sources of advice and help, and much more. Similarly detailed information is offered by Hearing Concern and Deafness Research UK. Other possible sources are listed at the end of the book. When we have to face up to the reality of our hearing loss it is comforting to know where to go, especially when the advice and information is so comprehensive and usually freely given.

Keeping a sense of proportion

While I hope that much of what you are about to read will provide an insight into what partial deafness has meant to me it can only be helpful if it gives you some confidence in being able to notice and understand the kind of problems that either you personally, or someone you care about, are likely to have to deal with. My hearing loss is highly unlikely to be the same as yours. For the same reason, don't worry that anyone about whose hearing you are concerned will share exactly the experiences that I have described.

Can you hear what I hear?

You may think you can but you cannot, not exactly.

Every hearing experience is very personal for each of us.

'Deaf' can never tell you how differently I hear.

John – *Is it my imagination?*

In the bright sunlight, I squint against the glare. Wind buffets me. I feel its cool. A sudden gust brings the smell of brine and a taste of salt from the sea. Yet it doesn't feel right. A whole dimension is missing. I am not involved, not properly connected. The sounds are not the same as the ones I remember.

Sound is physical and its effect is deeply emotional. Even though I may not notice their caress sound waves touch the whole surface of my body. I accept their vibrations as part of my consciousness. But with even a mild hearing loss, although my body still senses the physical presence, my ears do not deliver a clear sharp edge. The experience is muffled, like wearing a cloak of cotton wool. My whole being feels different.

Tricia – *So much taken for granted*

When I wake up in the morning, I become aware of all sorts of sounds; the birds singing, perhaps the wind blowing, or the patter of rain on the windows. There will be the noise of traffic outside, and on Sunday the church bells will peal. If there are other people in the house, there may be voices, music, the television or radio. The telephone might ring, or a door may slam. I can orientate myself by hearing what is happening, whether our daughter is in the shower, downstairs boiling the kettle, or getting out her breakfast crockery and cutlery.

As far as I can imagine, John wakes up enveloped in a blanket of nothing. There may be sounds inside his head but, until he puts on his hearing aid, he can have absolutely no conception of what is going on in the world. He may see the rain, or smell toast burning. He can notice what time it is and whether it is still dark or already daylight, but he cannot be conscious of many of the things that automatically start my day.

What's it like living with someone who is deaf?
Well, that depends on how deaf. If someone loses all their hearing, then you are facing a very definite problem. But when it creeps up on you, like it did with us, then it's more difficult. None of us could be quite sure how much of a problem it was, or how it was likely to develop. No point in ringing alarm bells unnecessarily. You don't want to make too much out of

little frustrations, in case by drawing attention to them you make things worse.

Having a hearing loss makes you self-conscious, even defensive. If people keep commenting, then your mindset is going to become negative, even if you don't want it to.

John – *Hard to be honest with myself*

'Right,' I answer. 'Good idea. Let's make sure we leave here before seven-thirty.'

She stares at me strangely. Nothing new in that. She shakes her head and mouths the words. 'Car keys?' I look blank. Her hands wiggle the imaginary steering wheel. 'You know, my car...?'

'I thought you said...' Just in time I stop. Not sure what I thought she'd said, but it definitely had nothing to do with her car, or its keys. As usual, I'm probably just not paying attention.

Patiently she asks: 'What did you think I said?'

'Just at that precise moment,' I answer very much on the defensive, 'I was thinking the traffic could be bad, and we don't want to be late, do we? Not like last time.'

'No, of course not.' Her eyes have that same searching, half-worried look I've been seeing quite a lot lately. 'Isn't it about time you had another hearing test?'

'Oh c'mon, I just wasn't concentrating.'

She's right though. Exactly what I've been thinking. Except there are some things you don't want to admit, even to yourself. Little incidents, like that last finance meeting with Marcus...

'As I'm sure you understand,' he told us from his big leather chair, with what I felt was unnecessarily heavy gravitas, 'the bank can only consider this kind of funding if you can give us the usual cup of tea.'

Hearing for John

I was concentrating on my figures. 'No problem,' I mutter without thinking. 'Debbie's remembered the Earl Grey, specially.' When I look up, faces around the table are staring at me very strangely, particularly Debbie. OK, let's run that one again. For medium term financing of one million pounds, the bank needs our usual cup of… Ahhh…Yeah, right! I put on my most reassuring grin. 'Of course!' I tell them, 'the guarantee.' Faces relax, except Marcus…

That was last week. But I can't pretend it was the first time.

She's still frowning thoughtfully. 'It's more than two years since you saw your consultant.' I bet she knows the exact date. 'He said you should go back at least once a year.'

True. But last time he did admit that the test could easily have been affected by the flight back from Australia. It wasn't a very encouraging consultation. He had quite a lot to say, but somehow not much went in. I kept pinching my nose and blowing. That's what used to make my ears pop. In the end I understood he wanted me to wait a week, and if they didn't clear, to come back. She's right, it has been more than two years. I stopped pinching my nose after a while. There were too many other things to do. Maybe he'll be able to suggest some other way to make them pop.

'Shall I book an appointment for you?'

'How can you? You don't know my diary,' I say ungraciously. 'I'll do it.'

'Really?' She doesn't think I will.

'You know how he told me that emotional pressures and tension could affect my hearing? Well, right now I

Hearing for John

have a load of pressure.' I don't sound very convincing, and her expression shows it. 'Just because I didn't hear you first time doesn't mean there's anything to worry about.'

She persists: 'I really wish you'd get it checked. The sooner the better.'

'It's my problem.'

'You're not the only one who has to live with it.'

She's right of course. My grandfather, who was almost totally deaf, was very difficult. In those days hearing aids were quite primitive. He tried one, hated it and, in disgust, hurled it into his overgrown Natal garden. After that he lived morosely in a world of his own – at least that's how it seemed to me. No enjoyment. No joy. No smile to lighten his severe, schoolmasterly face. It seemed that he just wanted to be left alone with his books, his beloved spaniel, Dandy, and a once-a-day walk to the post office to pick up letters, except Sundays.

Deafness took over his life. He struggled with the frustrations of trying to hear about the war and Hitler on the wireless. He turned up the volume to maximum. The nearest neighbours were well protected by lush green undergrowth and papaya trees, but I'm sure they heard more than he did, which is undoubtedly why the little flags on his large map of North Africa didn't seem to match the march of the campaigns as described by those distant BBC voices coming to him from the transmitters in Daventry. The wonderful restless pounding of the Indian Ocean surf, visible from his front garden, its voice always so strong, so much a part of my memories of his world, almost certainly didn't

Hearing for John

get through to him. Only now can I imagine how very much he must have felt isolated and alone. Could this be happening to me?

'OK. I'll book a test asap.' I mean it. Really.

And what if it shows that I have a problem? What if the prognosis is a long slippery slope into audio oblivion? What then?

Car keys magically emerge from the depths of her handbag. She glances at her watch, heads for the door. 'Won't be long. I'll make sure I'm ready to leave a lemon jersey.'

On reflection, I guess she must have said 'leave at seven-thirty'.

Tricia – *Has he really not heard me?*

Quite often I will ask him something and he will fail to reply. But sometimes, if I wait a bit rather than repeating it straight away, he will give a perfectly reasonable answer. Does this mean that (a) he thinks he's heard what I've said but feels it would be nice to have it confirmed; (b) his brain takes a bit longer to process my question because it needs to un-jumble and decode the sounds it has received; or (c) we have known each other for such a long time that he can guess virtually everything I am going to say? I do hope it's not (c).

Worse than having heard me and taking a bit of time to decode what I've said is not hearing me but indicating that he has. This can lead to recriminations later on when I say, 'But you said you would,' while he insists that I have never raised the subject. In theory it should give me carte blanche to do all sorts of things he might prefer I didn't but somehow I feel this could backfire most unpleasantly.

Probably one of the hardest things is having to repeat so much of what I say. It's not the repetition but the banality of my words which strikes me when I say them for the third time. If I'm asking him what time he wants lunch, fine, but if I'm just making an inconsequential remark I am reminded of my English teacher, who told us the story of a girl who was a great chatterbox. She was asked to consider three questions before opening her mouth. 'Is it kind?' It usually was. 'Is it interesting?' Yes to that too. 'But is it *necessary*?' Ah, probably not. And yet it is contact, connection, call it what you like, a way of sharing who we are, holding onto the comfortable feeling of being together.

John – *What my friends won't tell me*

Hearing loss is never easy. There is no point in trying to hide it or dodge its impact. We need to face it as honestly and practically as we can. And yet, at the same time, we want everything to be as normal as possible. Many people are very understanding and helpful once they recognise the problem, but there are always others who treat us with exaggerated care and concern in their well-intentioned efforts to spare our feelings.

'I… have… summ… thingg… to… showw… yooooo,' he mouths slowly and widely, while at the same time contriving an encouraging smile. He is trying to help me lipread. Show me? He holds out a familiar looking small package. Saw the advert and thought of me. Guaranteed to make my hearing normal. He has been very kind. He beams, waiting for my appreciation. Unfortunately I already know it won't work. I have exactly the same device in a drawer at home, with several other bits of optimistically promoted technology that have turned out to be disappointingly useless for my kind of hearing loss. He's doing his best to show me that he understands and wants to do anything he can to help. I have several other friends who also try. They make an extra effort whenever they are with me. Very warming.

Not so my grandchildren who, in their innocence, cannot be expected to humour my problem. Their unconsciously honest reactions are often very revealing. From them I have learned a great deal, which is what has prompted me to write a letter that each of them will receive when it seems to me that they are old enough to understand fully what it is trying to say. I am tempted to suggest that this letter may also give some helpful hints to more adult minds.

My dear ...,

I really enjoyed your birthday party yesterday. You and your friends are lots of fun. Did you see how some of them tried very hard to speak carefully and slowly to me? That was kind of them. Maybe they also have someone in their family who can't hear very well, so they know how it is for you.

Your smile, your bright eyes and your non-stop energy show me how wonderfully full of life you are. I have been trying to remember how I felt when I became ten years old. Like you I am sure I was very proud to get to double figures. Of course that was a long time ago. And yet you may be surprised to know that quite a lot of things were the same for me then as they are for you and me now.

I can remember how much I wanted to get through to my Grandad. He was quite a lot older than I am now and more deaf than I am. It was a very big problem for me. He was gruff and serious and never smiled. Even worse, I cannot remember a single time when he tried to talk to me. In the end, in my childish way, I worked out that he really didn't like me. For many years I had that idea. It was only when I was very much older, when I found that I had a similar problem with my hearing, that I began to understand how he must have felt, and why. He probably knew there was no point in trying to start any conversation with me if he couldn't hear me trying to answer him. As a result, he never knew me and I never knew him, which was a great shame for both of us. And that is why I want to do everything I can to make sure that you and I don't have the same problem now.

I can see how very hard you try to get through to me, and you show so clearly that you are disappointed and unhappy when, no matter what you do, I don't connect with you. You've been saving up specially to say those words. When I don't understand, Granny Tricia helps us by telling me what they are. But it isn't the same, is it? You want me to hear you. When I can't, we both lose something. You feel that you have failed. But I feel I have also failed.

I notice that sometimes you seem to be quite uncomfortable, and I've worked out that's because of the way I stare at you. There's a simple reason why I have to. If I can see the way your mouth is moving as you speak, and also if I can see the feelings you are showing in your eyes, I can usually decode your message. Lipreading is very important for me. And, if you watch me, you will see that I stare at everyone in the same way. I know it may seem rude, and this worries me. But I have to risk it. I really have no choice if I am going to do the best I can to understand you. Do you remember when you thought I was funny because I asked Granny Tricia to come out of the shadows when she was speaking to me? That was because I couldn't understand what she was saying until I could see her mouth moving.

You may be a bit frightened that I will ask you questions and then won't be able to connect sensibly with the answers that you give me. So you worry about how I will be, and I worry about how you will be, and we are both worrying because we feel it's our fault that we can't get through to each other. This is a terrible waste of worrying don't you think? Shouldn't we be trying instead to work out ways to make it better?

But how?

It's quite simple really. Neither of us should feel embarrassed, or guilty, or worried. Neither of us is to blame. There is no blame. The only thing we should both be thinking about is that Grandad hears differently from other people. You may wonder why I don't just say "Grandad is deaf." Well, although that is true, and we should never be afraid of the truth, I find that deaf sounds so final, which it isn't. It seems to make some people switch off – they can't be bothered to face up to the problems that they expect it will cause. So let's look at what's involved.

If we can't do something that everyone expects us to be able to do then some people will say that we are not normal. Of course in one way that's correct. But not normal also means that we are just different. And what's wrong with that?

We are all different in so many ways. Taller, shorter, darker, fairer, sporty, clever – there's no end to the list. We are none of us exactly the same as anyone else. If you think about it, this means that not a single human being anywhere is exactly 'normal'.

So where does this get us? Let's go back to how you think about my hearing loss. We can either say that your Grandad is deaf, or that he hears differently. Well if something is different, we have the challenge of learning what to do about it. Because I can't hear you very well, both you and I have to discover new ways to connect with each other. No shame in that. Quite the opposite, in fact. The more we try to handle the challenge together, the more we will have something to share and that will help us to learn more about each other. That's the nice part about a challenge. It gives us something to aim for, something to achieve. Best of all we can do it together.

There are times when I can see that we understand each other. But there are other times when you look confused, or worried, or just plain blank. This is always disappointing for me because it is clear that I haven't got through to you. It just makes me more determined than ever to try again.

This may explain why, whenever I have the chance, I try to talk to you. Even though I know it is difficult for both of us, I want to show you that bit by bit we can find our own special ways of getting through to each other. The more we do, the more we will understand each other. And that will help you to know, deep inside you, how very interested I am in you, and how I really enjoy every chance that we have to share things together. Always remember, that will never change no matter how much or how little I can hear.

Hearing for John

I have no doubt that, long before they read this letter, my grandchildren will have worked out for themselves how to deal with any problems my hearing loss causes them. But I want them to feel comfortable about sharing their thoughts with me because, over the years, I have discovered that my best hearing aids are people.

Samantha – *Never seems to bother him somehow*

I've never once thought of my dad as being disabled. That implies orange parking permits with wheelchair symbols. But I always knew he was different from other dads. It was a sort of unspoken difference – one which I was acutely aware of but never talked about. In fact, I didn't actually know if anyone else knew about it – if anyone else was in on the secret. For some reason I suspected that no-one other than us, his family, really knew. I hoped that my friends wouldn't notice despite the fact that he wore a hearing aid, two in fact, which in those days were nowhere near as discreet as the ones available now, so of course anyone would have noticed fairly quickly. But I tried to pretend that they didn't.

As far as I could see, other than the hearing aids, there was nothing noticeably different about him at all (maybe that's why I didn't think other people would necessarily realise). He looked normal, spoke normally and generally went about life in a normal way. But I knew that things were different. The way our house worked was different from the way my friends' houses appeared to work – it was quieter. As a result, I internalised things a lot, and still do. Now that may just be my nature, or the fact that I didn't have siblings of my own age, but I also think it may well have been because there wasn't the normal hustle and bustle, yelling and screaming (no bad thing really) that seemed to be the norm in other people's households. I didn't call down the stairs for him to come and look at something upstairs because he wouldn't hear. And there was no point in snide under-the-breath remarks because they would, quite literally, fall on deaf ears. So things were always quite polite really.

Dad's deafness in itself never worried me. Part of being a child is that you're not concerned with how things affect other people, just how they affect you. So the only time I'd get anxious or embarrassed was when my dad would meet my friends. I'd get nervous that he wouldn't hear them, or would mishear what they said and it would be embarrassing. In fact, embarrassment and fear of humiliation were the things that I associated with deafness. Strange really, as I never had any bad experiences to justify the fear, but the fact is that no child enjoys being different, which is what having a deaf dad made me feel. That and having horrid curly hair (which luckily Dad didn't share, otherwise that really would have been embarrassing).

These days, I am much more concerned about the possibility that he may be left out of conversations or feel that people will think it's too much of an effort to talk to him in a crowded, noisy environment where even those of us with normal hearing struggle. I tell friends beforehand if they're going to meet him that he doesn't hear well, and brief them to talk clearly and not cover their mouths while speaking. When I see him having a conversation with someone and I know that he can't see their lips clearly, I want to say something – to ask them to take their hand away from their mouth or to step into the light. But then

Hearing for John

again I don't want to interfere or, worse, act as if he needs looking after – he doesn't. But sometimes he needs an interpreter – a role into which both my mother and I fall quite naturally in social situations when we're with him.

John – *I will always have choices*

I have to be clear about my priorities. Staying connected means hearing and understanding what is said. That has to be the bottom line. I must learn to be happy with this modest but hugely valuable target. This comes home to me quite regularly, and in the most unexpected ways.

After a convivial Sunday lunch we were talking about plans for the coming summer. Son Guy had recently moved north from London to Leamington Spa and was enthusing about the flat he had bought. I was therefore surprised and a little alarmed when he added with a meaningful look in my direction: 'There won't be any ventilation from July.'

'Oh,' I answered cautiously, 'why ever not?'

'Why not what?' he demanded, clearly puzzled.

'The ventilation. Why won't it be working?' Even though he is fully grown up and fiercely independent, as a caring parent I feel that my continuing concern is not entirely out of place.

The family exchanged those knowing looks that have become so familiar to me.

Guy let me down gently. 'You didn't hear me did you?' I sensed a couple of smiling faces elsewhere in the room. 'What I said was, there'll be an open invitation from July.'

My brain can do a lot to make up for any shortcomings. It can be my most valuable supporter just as my sometimes negative attitude can be my most disloyal handicap. Attitude is the key. But it can be changed.

The more I recognise that most of the solutions (although admittedly not all of them) can be worked out inside my head, giving me a personal 'normality' good enough to interface with the normality that other people accept for themselves, the less I will feel at a disadvantage. Life offers unending options and it is my duty to myself to make choices that fit my changing circumstances rather than allowing myself to be locked in to the choices that other people expect me to accept.

This may mean some changes in lifestyle. It may also mean that I will (possibly with regret) turn my back on some of the situations and people I enjoy. Some of my older contacts and friends may come with me on this journey because our relationships are strong and because they value me as a 'total package' and are more than willing to help me deal positively with my hearing loss. Other people may fall away because they cannot be bothered to adjust to it. But that might have happened anyway. Instead of worrying about them going I should be thinking about what is new in my life so that I can make the choices that take me in hitherto unexplored, positive directions and allow me to build a future that suits my changed profile.

Something new is always interesting and exciting and with new contacts, colleagues and friends we can build our new normality which will do wonders for our confidence and self-respect. We have the freedom to create for ourselves a point of view that has realities and aims unique to us. We can build our world any

Hearing for John

way we choose as long as we are sure to remember our boundaries and do not feel any desperate need to match what many people regard as 'normality'. The crucial starting point is the great feeling of freedom that comes from recognising that we are unique (irrespective of how our hearing behaves) with our own, very individual version of normality.

Amanda – *He will never give up*

Independence has always been the flag that Dad has wanted us to salute because that is what he values in his own life. I have never known him to complain about his hearing loss. On the contrary, we are far more likely to be told about the latest settings he is trying in his most recently acquired state-of-the-art digital hearing aid. His enthusiasm for the technology that hearing professionals try for him knows no limits, and the fact that he has put this book together is typical of the very positive attitude he has always lived by.

He is not phased by the prognoses that have been regularly offered by hearing professionals who warn him of a steadily deteriorating future. And I remember clearly how infuriated he was by the doubtless well-intentioned audiologist who said that there was nothing more that he could do other than to recommend the name of a hearing therapist. I know that with his unflagging optimism he is convinced that sometime soon he will find something that will make our support less necessary. And yet he must be aware that, despite his determination to be independent, he is facing the need for increasing tolerance and help from friends and family. Whatever thoughts he has on this, he keeps to himself.

These days, as I watch him in social and family occasions, I can see how much he misses. This is especially important with anyone who has not worked out how to make the extra effort to get through to him. His grandchildren have that problem and it will

Hearing for John

be some years before they are old enough to grasp what is needed to sort out their own ways to make their connection with him work. However, there could be a bonus for them. I am quite convinced that the reason why I, and my brother Guy and my sister Samantha all speak so clearly is because we found that was the only we could get through to our Dad.

Because I know him so well and understand how he thinks, I always notice when the full meaning doesn't get through to him. It happens all too often. Typically, he will mishear words, but it is the undercurrent of meaning that he also misses. When someone repeats the words to make sure he connects with the subject, they may either fail to convey that undercurrent or even (which is worse) give things a different twist. Dad will not have been aware of the original subtle meaning so the connection does not work in the way that was intended. I used to wonder how often in his small, successful company people deliberately played on his difficulty to mislead him. I felt that I wanted to sit behind his shoulder as an interpreter to make sure he got the true picture.

John – *Sounds make sense of things*

What is it about hearing differently that causes us to worry and lose confidence? It is the fear of losing contact with recognisable hearing experiences we have had since childhood. When the sounds from familiar events change and become strange we may feel confused, disorientated. If we detect that we are 'missing things' we may decide we are being a bit slow, not as sharp as we should be. We may start to worry that other people will see us as losing our grip, and we may become anxious that we can no longer compete quite as well as we used to. This is especially upsetting when we can see from the reactions of other people that we haven't understood and connected with them. When they have to repeat things we may sense their frustration or irritation, and we may feel that they are losing respect for us which makes us lose respect for ourselves. Or when we see their sympathy we may feel awkward about accepting their sometimes clumsy – albeit well-intentioned – efforts to offer us help.

Being aware that we are not hearing sounds that would otherwise fill in the essential details of a picture can affect our confidence in our ability to handle situations correctly. The physical cut-off of hearing loss can make us feel deprived and isolated, all the more when we can see what is going on and yet are not able to understand what is involved. There is also the feeling that we may not be able to respond adequately to people and will therefore lose their acceptance of us as equal partners in the contact.

Hearing for John

The spoken word works on so many different levels all of which are transmitted simultaneously. We not only hear words. The tone of voice and the speed of delivery add very definite extra messages. Even pauses between phrases can be loaded with meaning. Miss them, and we possibly miss the most important part of the connection.

Even if all the visual clues are unambiguous and seem easy to understand, missing or mishearing important words or phrases or failing to detect an emotional undertone may change the whole way we perceive a situation and lead to misunderstandings. The consequences can be complicated, although sometimes quite humorous.

One example is typical. At the end of a river cruise that had lasted several days I asked for my bill early to make sure that none of the crew members who had looked after us so very well had been left out of the usual gratuities.

Most of them were Hungarian which perhaps made it harder than usual for me to understand what they were saying. But it still came as something of a shock when the purser said: 'You can only keep the cabin key until you leave the tip.'

I had assumed that we would be free to continue using the cabin until our departure after breakfast. My pen, poised to fill in a figure for gratuities on the credit card slip, froze. 'That's a bit pushy,' I muttered to myself. 'Bloody nerve!'

Tricia was beside me and, with her antenna ever alert to my changes of mood, asked quietly: 'Anything the matter?'

'Hear what he said?' I demanded curtly.

She nodded. 'Keep the key until you leave the ship. Anything wrong with that?'

How critical is this problem? Think of a suburban street with a row of identical houses. Visually there is no difference between them. However from one comes the noise of a party while next door a burglar alarm is ringing. Those sounds are the only clues we have to guide us. Without hearing them what's at stake? If we go into the wrong one, instead of joining the party to which we have been invited we may find ourselves innocently involved in a criminal break-in. It is even more relevant with people. At a pavement café in Paris two people are talking intimately. In every way they appear to be French until we get close enough to discover that they are speaking Russian. Without hearing them we would have made the wrong assumptions. Sounds give us the full meaning of all our experiences.

Hearing is different from all the other senses because it goes right to the core of our feelings and is a vital part of the emotional lifeline that connects us to other people. They like to see that we can quickly and easily tune into their wavelength. It reassures them that they are getting through. When we have difficulties it may appear that we are being standoffish or at best missing the point. Are we being a bit dim or should they worry about how badly they are communicating? Either way the contact is not working. They, and we, are having a problem accepting each other.

The way someone speaks to us can trigger various feelings depending on the character and emotion that we hear. Affectionate words softly spoken can make us feel loved and warm. Angry demands may raise our hackles or cause us to feel fear. Intolerant threats will either make us nervous or attract our contempt. However, hearing loss can prompt quite different reactions, some of them mistaken, because there is less clarity, even a feeling of barrier. Getting through it may need time, patience and understanding. In today's 'rush-rush' world these are, more often than not, in very short supply.

Even with perfectly normal hearing, people regularly find themselves wrong-footed by misunderstandings. Has the speaker not made the meaning clear? Or is it because, even though we hear the words plainly, other thoughts already in our mind have given everything a twist?

This is where, ironically, my hearing loss can be both a challenge and also, quite frequently, an advantage. I have grown used to doing everything I can to make sure I understand what is going on. I don't hesitate to ask speakers to repeat what they have said, not only once but enough times for me to be certain that I have read them correctly. I probably concentrate on them with more focus than a listener with normal hearing.

Do I get the whole meaning? Or do I only have the bare bones of the words that don't convey the subtleties that are so often at least as important as the words themselves? I need confirmation in a way quite different from someone with no hearing loss. This is where the practice I have had in focusing on eyes, face and body language helps me to fill in the gaps. When this works my connection becomes more perceptive and personal and the chances of misunderstanding are reduced.

Hearing for John

With experience I have learned how to make people feel that I have heard and understood even when, although I can hear the sound of their voice, it has not been possible to decode the actual words, so their meaning is lost to me. This happens especially often when the background noise is high. Voices merge into the general din. They become just one more noise. But if I can pick up one or two words and if I know the person who is speaking reasonably well I can have a pretty accurate guess at what they are saying. It works remarkably well. They don't feel frustrated about not getting through and I can feel good about succeeding with my aural guessing game.

The problem that most usually upsets this neat little scenario is a discontinuity – when someone changes the subject and I miss the one or two key words that would tell me what has happened. From this point and until I can decode another key word I won't have a clue what is going on. But it usually doesn't matter. And it is far more important that others are able to continue their conversation naturally without having to make special allowances for me. It really can be quite good for my self-respect because it helps me to believe that I can operate in a dimension that is as natural as possible.

Tricia – *A little bit of history*

Being deaf must be a bit like knowing a foreign language quite well but not quite well enough. You are in a group of people having a lively conversation and are managing just fine, missing some of the words but keeping up with the gist of it. And then suddenly someone switches the subject. And you have no idea what is going on. You try desperately to get hold of a key word. Or maybe you don't even realise that the subject has changed and think everyone is still enjoying being nasty about Tony Blair. 'The sooner he goes the better,' you say cheerfully. And then you become aware of someone muttering agitatedly into your good ear that actually they are now talking about Margaret's husband who has just been diagnosed with terminal cancer.

Then there are times when you cannot get any idea whatsoever of what is going on. At the end of a jolly evening John was having a lively conversation with two of the guests when he looked to me for help. The indecipherable word for him, I discovered, was 'caterpillar'. I got it through to him and the conversation continued with much hilarity.

Next morning I said to John, 'What was all that about caterpillars?'

'Haven't the faintest idea,' he replied.

John could hear perfectly well when I first met him. True he got the odd ringing in his ears but he put that down to the copious amounts of aspirin he took to get him started on hangover days. However, his father was a bit deaf as was his mother and his mother's sister.

Hearing for John

His grandfather had ended up totally deaf. It was not unreasonable therefore to assume that deafness would run in the family

As a BBC television producer he covered quite a lot of Formula One World Championship Grand Prix. In those days ear defenders were a comparatively rare sight in the pits. At Monaco, Monza and Nurburgring, and also at the Le Mans 24 hour sports car races his ears would be subjected to several hours of deafening, unrelenting roar as he worked with the film crews as close as possible to the trackside. After each one it took longer and longer for his hearing to regain anything like its former normality but when he mentioned this to a BBC doctor he was told it was extremely unlikely that there was any connection.

In the end he began to feel seriously concerned and after a difficult weekend in Vienna with two good friends he decided that he was going to have to get a hearing aid.

John – *Sooner or later I had to...*

Decision made. The die is cast. Willingly? Not really. But probably no going back.

Last weekend finally did it. No-one minds repeating the odd word or two. But when small talk has to be spelled out, it loses its spice. 'Funny' doesn't work if it has to be explained. They did their best to help but most of the time a blank look from me was the only reward they got for their efforts. Not like it used to be. Frustrating and exhausting for all four of us. No fun. And now it's on my mind all the time, at work, at home, even while I'm out shopping.

My box of eggs passed the magic eye with a beep. I fumbled with my cash card as she waited. Then just as she put the card into the chip-and-pin reader there was a shattering noise. Heads everywhere swivelled. Mine too, except I looked the wrong way. The girl was mildly amused. I changed my focus to follow her gaze. Someone had demolished a display of wines on special offer.

I blinked at her. 'Sorry. What did you say?'

'Crash-hat,' she repeated with one eye on the chaos, even though the broken bottles and burgundy were not her problem. 'Do you want a crash-hat?' I could see in her eyes that she had no idea why she couldn't get through to me. How many times a day does she ask the same simple question? Why no answer?

I blinked again. Is this some kind of promotion? Maybe a new kind of giveaway for cyclists? Supermarkets are doing everything they can to promote their green image. But with this pile of shopping do I look like I came on two wheels?

I shook my head. 'Sorry. I'm very deaf.'

'Cash back,' she mouths more carefully.

Got it at last. I really don't connect like I used to. Yep, it's gone on too long. I try to be a player but I'm only in half the game. Whole chunks are missing. They can see I'm trying and they're kind enough – up to a point. But why should they bother?

My consultant used his sympathetic 'nothing to worry about' voice. He made it sound so normal. Obviously in his mind it's no big deal. Nothing really exceptional about my hearing loss. It's typical. Except typical is just a very convenient label. They use it a lot. It ignores an important reality. We are all individual and very different. Typical is a blanket that covers up – smothers more like it – the very personal character of my hearing loss. Will it get worse? Can't say (he clearly believes it will). How much worse? Well let's put it this way: I should appreciate how lucky I am because the technology is moving so fast it will be getting better even though I may be getting worse. That's a real bonus don't you see? Hearing aids are improving all the time, quite small and unobtrusive, nothing like the old days. Of course it's down to me. No-one can force me to wear them. But if I want to improve my life there's no real alternative. I'll get used to them he tells me. Plenty of people do.

Should I trust him? Can I afford not to? That's the whole point with doctors, isn't it? I'm not supposed to doubt him. He has knowledge – and knowledge is power (who said that?). The relationship is always going

Hearing for John

to be unequal. I don't like this feeling. Never again can I be totally in control, not if I'm going to need him and other people like him for the rest of my life.

Why do I feel negative? What's so terrible about putting a bit of plastic in my ear if it's going to make a difference? Easy. I just don't think I'm going to like it very much. Whatever he says a hearing aid can never be small enough, unobtrusive enough, socially acceptable enough for me. Maybe I'll grow my hair longer to hide my ears. What else can I do? It's all very confusing. And worrying? Yeah, you could say that.

But it's going to make everything a lot better – that's what it says in the adverts. Free trial. If it doesn't work for me I can give it back. I'm the customer. I have the choice. So why do I have this nagging worry? Because suddenly I have to face it. I can't any longer put it down to not paying attention or having selective hearing. No doubt about it. I have a real hearing loss. How bad is it?

When he did the test I didn't do nearly as well as two years ago. As usual I sat in his completely soundproof booth and pressed the button whenever I could hear various beeps, some low and others high. Problem was I couldn't be sure if I was hearing beeps or if they were just noises in my head. Guessed some. Quite difficult because, to check how well I hear them, he changes the loudness of each one. They start quite clearly and then fade away. His machine shows him the points at which the softest beeps are audible for me. He calls them thresholds. From them he plots the audiogram graph. It's pointing downwards much more steeply than last time. I've lost a lot of my high frequencies he tells me.

Hearing for John

They are typically the first to go. But the loss is quite severe. It's bound to affect my speech recognition.

Is this why I keep making these silly bloopers? Like that final evening in Spain when we were trying to decide where to go for one last meal.

'How about somewhere beside the sea?' I proposed, hoping that delicious aromas and flavours would blend unforgettably with salty wafts on a cool evening breeze. 'La Nueva Reina?'

'Closed on Mondays,' she reminded me.

'Ah yes,' I agreed. 'Shame. It would have been perfect.' We dawdled along in silence. Then I pointed. 'What about that one?' Pause. 'No. Maybe not. Something tells me we didn't like it last time. Remind me?'

Her answer was unhesitating. 'All flies.'

I stopped and stared. 'Surely,' I protested, 'it wasn't that bad? Come to think of it I don't remember any flies at all.'

Her face was a mixture of amusement and sympathy. 'All fries,' she said kindly. 'Too much batter and oil.'

The consultant has given me a letter and I've made the appointment with the hearing aid audiologist. Next Thursday.

Professional – *Breaking the ice*

Some people can be very reluctant to admit they've lost the ability to hear quite as well as they used to be able to. They don't want to accept that they've got a problem. Often that's because it's been developing very gradually. It's usually family or friends who have pointed it out to them. They feel anxious; sometimes they are angry. If the hearing loss has been sudden they can be very upset – they've got the comparison of hearing normally a short while ago and not hearing now

The information from the basic audiogram indicates the type of loss – whether it's mild, moderate or severe, and what frequencies the patient is missing. There are other tests, including a speech test, which tell us a bit more about how the ears are interpreting all the different signals and mixed frequencies.

I feed the information from the audiogram into a computer which works out the kind of settings that the tiny processor in a digital hearing aid needs to compensate for a particular pattern of hearing loss. Generally we're interested in the speech frequency range. High frequency losses that make it difficult to hear the treble sounds are most common. They cause problems with consonants, and sounds like 'f', 's', and 'th' are not heard as loudly or as clearly as 'm', 'e', or 'j' sounds.

Manufacturers have developed algorithms to convert the information from the audiogram into a form that the hearing aid can use. Different manufacturers have worked out different ways of converting and processing

Hearing for John

that information, and that's why not all hearing aids are the same.

The tests give you a very good idea of what you can do with a hearing aid, but it's difficult to predict how much benefit the patient will get because hearing losses are always slightly different for everyone.

John – *My big learning curve*

'Understand you're thinking of getting a hearing aid? Great stuff.' He's been part of my working life for some years but we never socialise.

'They've talked me into it,' I nod sheepishly. 'Try anything once.' I really feel quite embarrassed. Why?

'I'm sure you won't regret it,' he muses. 'Look I hope you won't take this the wrong way. We've been noticing how hard it is for you especially in meetings. We know it's not your fault. But to be honest we've been wondering why you haven't thought about getting one long before now.'

Haven't thought about it? Does he know what he's saying? It's the one thought I've been trying not to think about. It's been getting in the way of a whole lot of other much more important thoughts. Even my golf swing? Yeah, even that. Just shows what it's doing to me. And now, all of a sudden, they're on my case. My hearing has become a matter of great concern to them. Actually they're not concerned. They're just fed up with having to explain and repeat things to me. If I was a puppy they would probably send me for house-training to stop my muddles making messes in the middle of their clever conversations. They want me sorted. You can say I am being super-sensitive but this just proves that I'm definitely not in control and the worst part is I don't know what to do about it.

'Don't hold your breath,' I caution. 'Not too sure how much good it's going to do.'

Hearing for John

'Oh c'mon,' he urges. 'you need to be more positive surely? Mind over matter. If you fight, you'll win. I guarantee it. And we're right behind you.'

That's exactly what's worrying me. Do I need them riding shotgun on my life? I face him squarely. 'What bothers you most – when I mess up what you are saying to me or when I don't hear you at all?'

The question shocks him. 'Nothing bothers me,' he answers earnestly. 'Can't you understand that we are worried about you? We really are. When you get the wrong end of the stick you can't possibly keep your thinking straight can you? Even though it's not your fault the result is the same. Sometimes it's a total screw-up.'

Sensitive and supportive isn't he? Just the sort of bloke I need in my corner. I know I should be grateful that he's being honest. Tough questions need tough answers. Better than dodging a load of little lies that only make things worse. Even so it's obvious that he and they really don't know or care about the cause, only the way it affects them.

What they don't realise is that I can't make it better until I know what I am really up against. This isn't some kind of challenge that I can get into training for. I'm not in a race where I can see the winning tape. There's no flag ahead of me on the putting green. In fact I really don't have a clue what kind of game I'm in. And until I can work it out I'm not going to be able to play or fight or do anything that means a row of beans – whatever he says.

I need facts – realities that will help me to understand. No point in asking friends and family, never mind my frustrated work colleagues. They don't know any more than I do. Hearing loss is one of those awkward things that you don't chat about to enjoy yourself. And anyway it's never going to be a burning issue for them because it's hard to understand, and invisible. I need to do some serious homework. Where do I start?

How about **sound**? That's what I'm missing. Words, music, noises have been part of my life forever. But what makes them happen? And how do I hear them? This doesn't need deep research, just some easy-to-understand facts.

Sound first. Anything that disturbs the air – maybe the beat of a drumstick, the exhaust of a car, or the vocal chords of my voice – creates vibrations that travel outwards in sound waves. When I watch a distant golfer drive off from a tee the noise of club hitting ball does not reach me instantly. There is a mini-delay while the vibrations which become sound waves take time to 'swim' through the air.

Sound waves contact not only my ears but the whole surface of my body. As I hear them I also feel them. When they are powerful enough – the roar of a racing car, the pounding beat of music, the ear-shattering thunder of an explosion – they give me a total experience that is both mental and physical. At a disco party, one of the women caught everyone's attention with her extraordinary dancing. I was one of the few guests who knew how exceptional her achievement was. She is profoundly deaf! She keeps to the beat by sensing the vibrations. Quieter sounds don't make the same noticeable impact on my body even though they are touching me all the time.

Hearing for John

The world is alive in so many different ways, and most of them cause vibrations. In some remote, wonderfully peaceful place in the countryside I may believe I am surrounded by silence. But I'm not. An important part of my enjoyment is the presence of an atmosphere that contains a whole tapestry of tiny vibrations, a crucial extra dimension of sounds some of which are too soft to be audible. Without them my experience would be completely different. The 'life' would not be there, more like looking at a painting or photograph, and I would notice the loss.

But how does my **hearing** work?

When sound waves arrive in my ear canal they cause the eardrum to vibrate and three small and very delicate bones in my middle ear move. The vibrations go deeper into the inner ear – the cochlea – which is filled with fluid in which tiny hair cells are immersed. When vibrations disturb the fluid the hair cells move and generate signals in the auditory nerve which takes them into my brain.

If those signals are familiar and match any of my memories created by earlier sound inputs I accept them without question and my reactions are automatic. But when a sound is new, and does not trigger any memories that match, I will be curious to know what it is. As soon as I discover what caused it, and understand what it is, it becomes just another memory so that the next time I will accept it without any hesitation.

Normal hearing is mostly an automatic reaction to sound signals that are familiar and resonate with experiences that are already in our memory. But when we have to get used to hearing loss many of the signals

Hearing for John

are unfamiliar and we have a whole new learning process to go through, rather like living in a different world of sounds. This may explain why, with someone who has problems hearing, we regularly see in their eyes a question mark as they try to work out the meaning of what they are hearing even though the sounds may be quite normal and ordinary.

Persistent exposure to loud or aggravating sounds can not only be emotionally stressing; it can also cause lasting and irreversible damage to the ear itself. Guns and explosives, machines, open exhausts and excessively loud music are some of the culprits and, although health and safety regulations now try to build in safeguards, there are still many everyday noises that put our hearing severely at risk, especially if we ignore advice to use well-designed ear defenders.

The ear has an amazing ability to compensate for extremes of sound and most of the time it smoothes out the most severe impacts on our hearing. But this flexibility and resilience has unfortunate side-effects. It allows us to believe that we can tolerate those extremes and it disguises the damage they can do. Many of today's disco junkies, driven by the excitement of maximum decibels, will have to deal with hearing problems sooner rather than later in life. The use of firearms either for military or sporting purposes has been blamed for deafness in middle age for many users who did not have the protection of ear defenders that only came into general circulation towards the end of the twentieth century. There is no shortage of other hazards and too little is being done to promote awareness of the risks among people who have yet to develop significant hearing problems. Unlike better-publicised addictions that can very often be remedied – alcohol, cigarettes, drugs – abuses of sound have consequences that are less obvious and yet impossible to reverse. Sadly this message has not been given the importance that it deserves. Once damaged, the delicate mechanisms of the ear can seldom be repaired and restored to normal health.

With damaged hearing my brain doesn't receive all the information that my ears are designed to supply. It's as though there's a kind of filter stopping me from experiencing all the clear sharp signals that should give me the full sounds I have grown up to expect – in some ways similar to the limited taste of sucking through a straw instead of savouring the complete experience of a mouthful from a cup or a glass. Is this what a hearing aid is going to fix for me? Will it unblock my ears? Will I get the full taste of all those sounds again?

'I hope very much,' I say cautiously, 'that if it works you will notice the difference. But if it doesn't, I'll just have to do something else.' I try to look cheerful. 'Maybe you can pass me your messages on bits of paper in a forked stick.'

He is not amused. 'You won't give up will you? It's too important.'

'I will do the best I can,' I assure him. 'That's all I can promise.' I pick up the newspaper. 'Maybe I'll get one of these.'

I show him the story about American space scientists who have already had some success with sensors tapping into the electrical impulses in the brain that prepare the words we want to say. The idea is to make it possible

Hearing for John

for astronauts to transmit their 'unspoken thoughts' without opening their mouths or making any sound. What a fantastically total rethink that may cause in communication and hearing. But until it's in the shop window for people like me I can only hope that hearing aids will continue to get better.

He should be impressed. 'Interesting idea,' he mumbles. Clearly, it's not. Not for him. Why? Because he really doesn't understand the problem. He has no idea what it feels like to be cut off. 'Lucky bastard,' I mutter under my breath. 'Good hearing you can take for granted, until you no longer have it.'

One thing I am absolutely sure about. Hearing is all very personal. Each one of us is affected in a different way. It is therefore misleading and wrong for us to be pigeon-holed inside a box marked 'typical' no matter how convenient that may be from a clinical or commercial or social point of view. We should ignore the word and be cautious about people who label us with it.

Tricia – *Our noisy world*

We are unendingly assaulted by noise. The cinema offers wraparound volume that shakes your seat. A car drives past with its radio or CD player pulsing heavily (is it safe to drive like this?). At discos, no chance to chat because the beat is blasting walls and ears the way punters like it. In pubs and restaurants you struggle to be heard above the 'background' music. Private parties are the same. Shops massage us with muzak to help our buying decisions – silence won't put us in the right mood. In my dance studio – average age 50+ – the music is so loud it hurts my eardrums and continues deafeningly afterwards with most people apparently unaware of its existence as they sip their coffee. Bombard us with high level sound. Make us feel we are having a good time.

Except, many of us enjoy silence. I don't need to be wrapped in sound as an add-on to reading or socialising. But, sadly in my view, silence is no longer golden. On the contrary, people seem to need the reassurance of constant noise. Take a normal suburban commuter train. Most of the occupants who aren't shouting into their mobiles are plugged into their Mp3 players into which they have proudly downloaded 3,500 different bits of music. Therefore if you don't happen to be doing either of these your journey is punctuated by a mixture of tinny emissions from the Mp3 players and a competition by the guard and the mobile users updating you on how much longer it's going to take to get to Waterloo and which station you're coming to next.

Hearing for John

When people say a noise is deafening do they realise the literal implications? Do they have any idea how vulnerable our ears are to any excesses of sound? It's only recently that men using pneumatic drills were given ear defenders, ditto on the Grand Prix circuit. With the nanny state legislating wildly on our safety in all directions, stopping little boys from playing conkers, banning hanging baskets in the high street and exhorting us to read everything on the label of a yoghurt pot, why are there no regular high profile government health warnings about the dangers of the steadily growing noise nuisance?

Would a health warning help John? Probably not, although any reduction in nuisance noise would make it easier for him to decode the words and sounds that are important for him. But any publicity promoting more urgent action to reduce the damage, most of it incurable, that excessive noise can do to the delicate mechanisms of the ear might help people who now have normal hearing to avoid having to cope later in their lives with the quality of hearing that John deals with today.

By the way I enjoy music. But when I listen to it I want to give it my full attention – I believe it deserves that.

John – *Devils in the decodes*

The hearing aid audiologist has a comfortable office with desk, computer, and a wash basin in the corner. Definitely relaxed. We chat and the words he uses are simple and direct. He's going to work out which hearing aid will be best for me. Digital has changed everything. There are quite a lot of options. Different makes with different features. He doesn't go into a lot of detail. I can't be expected to understand the finer points. He will recommend.

First, another hearing test. No soundproof booth this time. Instead, connected to his pure tone audiometer, he uses chunky headphones that keep out unwanted sounds. The beeps are the same. They come and go, and again I have a few fairly hopeless guesses and press the response button almost at random especially with the high sounds. Does he know? Can he call my bluff? I hope so. I need to trust him. At this point does everyone else feel as confused as I do right now?

The result looks exactly the same. The curve of the audiogram goes south like it did with the consultant. At least they seem to be working from the same song sheet. Same jargon. My upper frequencies are missing.

Next, something different. He is going to check how well I recognise words. With normal hearing we automatically use the lessons of a lifetime to link vowels and consonants into familiar words no matter how fast or slowly they are spoken. More remarkably we usually manage to do this very well even when a speaker has

Hearing for John

a strong accent that makes some of the words almost unrecognisable.

Once again I put on the headphones. I will listen to a list of words and say out loud what I think I am hearing:

Headphones	'Hush'	Me	'Rush?'
Headphones	'Gas'	Me	'Guess?'
Headphones	'Thin'	Me	'In?'
Headphones	'Fake'	Me	'Fake?'
Headphones	'Chime'	Me	'Time?'
Headphones	'Weave'	Me	'Eve?'
Headphones	'Dope'	Me	'Dope?'

There are more, but the result is not very good.

Hearing is our ability not only to detect but also to decode sounds. It's important to remember the difference between the two. I can often hear all the sounds made by a speaker at a meeting, the actors on a stage, or a caller on the telephone and yet may not decode what they are saying. 'Heard everything, understood nothing' plays a big part in my life. Clearly word recognition seems to be my Achilles heel.

Detecting sound is a physical experience. But it's the other half of the story that creates communication. Decoding is largely a question of memory. Usually there is no conscious thought. Our brain matches the sound that is incoming now with memories of similar sounds that we have experienced earlier in our lives, and those memories cause us to react 'automatically'. For example the sound of the word 'no' – which is similar

Hearing for John

in many languages – restrains us, makes us hesitate or stop completely because we have learned from previous experiences that is what we should do when we hear it. But our understanding of more complex words and phrases always depends upon how closely the word-sounds that our ears offer to our brain match our embedded memories. Because of my hearing loss today's word-sounds will be different from the ones that originally created my memories of the same words, and as a result my brain's recognition and decoding will not work as well as it used to.

A good way of understanding problem is to watch a live TV broadcast with sub-titles working in real time. The computer driven word recognition systems that generate sub-titles have become remarkably accurate and appear to be getting better all the time – doubtless because of the word recognition experiences that they are accumulating daily. Their biggest difficulties seem to come from words or phrases that do not instantly match any of the data already stored in the system memory. A few simple examples:

Sub-title:	Reality:
'Alexander living gingko'	'Alexander Litvinenko'

Sub-title:	Reality:
'age of a diamond'	'age of retirement'

Sub-title:	Reality:
'corporation of the Russians'	'co-operation of the Russians'

Hearing for John

Watching these and other confusions gives me a comfortable 'been there done that' feeling.

Noises in general need to be interpreted accurately. The sound of an engine approaching tells me that some kind of machine will soon be with me. I can approximately decode the direction from which the machine is approaching and the speed. My conditioning gets me ready to take avoiding action if necessary. However, this decoding has also been changed by my hearing loss. The volume will be different for a start and I will not get the information as quickly and as clearly as I did when my hearing was normal. More importantly the character of the sound may be unexpected which will trigger different memories and therefore different reactions in me.

So that we can react to sounds 'normally' in the way we learned from earlier experiences we have to relearn our decoding. This is not as difficult as it may seem if we remember that it is entirely possible for us to change the way we think. Sadly too often many of us give up. 'Can't hear that any more,' is a total negative. A more positive attitude says, 'This sounds different. Perhaps for me all engines will sound like this in future.'

I wait as he washes his hands very thoroughly. I can sense a change of tempo. Now for the first time he uses an instrument, an otoscope, which will allow him to peer into my ears. What for? Wax. If there's too much he won't be able to take an impression of the ear canal for the ear mould. I'll have to go back to my GP for a syringe job to clear it out. Only doctors can do this (or in the case of my GP, the practice nurse). He's not a doctor.

Hearing for John

'Hmm! Let's look at the other one.' An anxious pause. Yup. Both ears are OK. That's a relief. Now what?

He rolls a lump of pink paste between his fingers and loads it into a shiny oversize syringe. He asks me to offer my left ear. Into it he drops a little bobble attached to a short piece of ribbon. It tickles slightly. With careful precision he aims the syringe into the ear canal and squeezes slowly. Again a mild tickle as the paste fills the empty space. He gently taps it with his forefinger to make sure it fills up snugly. Now we wait while it sets.

His choice of wall art is limited. No placid reassuring landscapes. Instead, two large luridly coloured diagrams show the workings of the ear. In amongst all the indicator arrows and notations I recognise the word 'cochlear'. I squint to see if those delicate little hair cells are visible. Can't see from where I'm sitting. Not much point in asking either. Won't be able to hear what he says because with no hearing in my right ear and with the paste in the left no sound is getting through to me. I am experiencing what it must be like to have no hearing at all. Lightly he taps it again to see if it has hardened. A few more seconds and then the whole purpose of the bobble and ribbon becomes clear. A gentle tug on the ribbon pulls the paste out of my ear. Sound floods in again as he studies the weird shape that has hardened inside the canal.

'Hmm!' He nods, satisfied. This is it then. This is what the insides of my ears look like – not all the way in mind you – an exact shape that the technicians need to make the all-important mould. It has to fit perfectly

Hearing for John

otherwise there may be feedback (more jargon) that will spoil the performance of the hearing aid. With the latest digital aids there's much less risk of that happening.

A few more polite remarks and I'm excused with an appointment card for Thursday next week when the ear mould will have come back from the technicians and, for the first time, I will sample the technological miracle that will change my life. Difficult not to feel impatient. A week passes soon enough but somehow I want it now even though I appreciate this is not possible.

Any questions? Yeah, plenty. Just can't seem to remember them all right now. And anyway, what difference will they make? I'll make a list and have them ready for next Thursday.

Professional – *It's all about trust*

People usually have preconceptions of what hearing aids are like and what they can and can't do. Some of them assume that as soon as they put a hearing aid on they will get normal hearing back. Of course it's not like that.

That's why at the beginning I try to concentrate on helping them to understand what is possible and what they can expect. Maybe they've seen publicity in the press, maybe they've heard from other people what digital hearing aids can do and the information is not always correct. It's important to give them the facts.

There's a big range or hearing aids available. Some are quite basic and others have really very advanced features. I try to recommend one that suits not only the patient's degree of loss but also the kind of life they want to lead. That's why it is important for me to understand something about their background – not in great detail but enough to get an idea about their individual environments. For example if they work do they deal face-to-face with other people, how much do they need to use the telephone, or do they have a lot of important meetings? Maybe they're retired, go to a lot of social situations, enjoy theatre and concerts, play a lot of sport or go to church – things like that. I find that as people get more comfortable with me they automatically start to fill in the details.

As far as possible I try to build up an ongoing relationship with them because their hearing can change or their lifestyle may change putting them in different work or social environments where the original settings of the hearing aid don't work quite so well. My experience has taught me that one of the most important things is to have a comfortable understanding between the hearing professional and the patient. It may take a bit of time to develop but it is the only way we can really appreciate what kind of difficulties we are facing so that we can find the best solutions.

So it's a whole package, not just a question of feeding settings from the computer into a hearing aid, giving it to the patient in a box and off they go. Unfortunately I know of people who have gone abroad to get a hearing aid and that has literally happened. They've received the hearing aid in the post and they've had to find out for themselves what to do, where to put it, how to adjust it. You really can't fit hearing aids without the counselling side that gives information about what to expect and how to cope with the problems that will always come up.

John – *Great expectations*

Memories of my introduction to each of the hearing aids that have been prescribed for me are all very similar. In every case I have had a sense of anticipation even excitement. And then, when I hear the sounds that the instrument produces, I have mixed emotions as I try to decide how well it is working for me. By nature I always hope for the best and imagine how perfectly things are going to turn out. In describing my feelings I often tend to be a bit dramatic. So don't let my stories put you off. Your reactions are unlikely to be quite the same. You may even take to using a hearing aid without any question marks whatsoever. Many people do. We all have our own individual ways of dealing with anything new.

There it is sitting on the desk inside a neat smart shock-proof box. Don't know exactly what I was expecting. But it looks somehow different from what I have seen in the ears around me. Small? That's what I want, isn't it? Hide it if I can. I want to be normal, don't I?

To begin with he doesn't do much explaining. He stands beside me and gently works the mould into the ear. Feels like a good fit. He clips a wire to the hearing aid from a loop that he has put around my neck. He needs it to connect the aid to his computer. He switches on. A flood of sound. Not the kind of noises I am used to. But on the other hand plenty of them. Traffic passes outside the window. I hear it faintly even through the double-glazing. There is a new presence all around me

Hearing for John

– like being in a big hall? No, not exactly, but that's the closest I can think of. I guess that's because there's a lot more sound than I have been used to lately. His voice is louder. Too loud? Maybe, a touch. It's a different voice. I sound different. Do I mean better? Not sure. All a bit strange. Not natural exactly. But then I probably shouldn't expect that.

A digital hearing aid has a built-in highly sensitive micro-processor designed to think for itself and react in the best way to give me maximum support with my hearing loss. It will not only help me to adjust to loud or quiet sounds. It will also detect the difference between the calm countryside and the chaos of a rowdy party. It may allow me to make my own small adjustments or it may be programmed to do the whole job without any input from me. It is designed to be a partner for my brain. And, in the ways it can be programmed to make its own decisions about how to feed sounds into my ear, it has a personality of its own.

I wonder how much impact that may have on me?

However, although the digital system is very clever, it has limitations. It cannot possibly discern how my hearing loss has altered my reactions to any single sound or group of sounds compared with the uniquely personal emotions they generated in me in the past. The total experience of hearing (not just the frequencies) can never be a precisely measurable quantity. It's not like watching the speedometer in a car or checking my weight on the bathroom scales. That's because the 'electrical' process – sound waves sending signals to my brain – is only the beginning.

Hearing for John

Matching those signals with embedded memories is always personal. Cannot be anything else. Even though most of them are very ordinary and I take them for granted – cups and cutlery, car engines, barking dogs, telephones – there are other sounds that can give me an emotional shiver as they 'touch a nerve'. They trigger in my memory earlier experiences that were exciting, pleasurable or perhaps scary. Musicians deliberately arrange combinations of harmonies and instruments to generate feelings and moods that we will experience in a special way because of our memories. The emotional effect they have is not easy to describe much less measure. And if, due to our loss, we hear the combination of instruments and harmonies differently our emotions cannot possibly be the same as they were in earlier times. We have completely individual memory banks and different sounds in different combinations open very different doors, all of them unique to each of us.

Hearing is a total happening. When the ear no longer works 'normally', parts of that happening no longer happen for us. With some sounds no longer clear, with changed emphasis on various frequencies, our memory receives different codes. When they don't match what we are expecting, we feel confused, disorientated, often frustrated.

Manufacturers of hearing aids, and the professionals who sell them and fit them, understand very well how parts of our daily experiences lose their potency as our ability to hear the full range of sounds decreases. They can set up the aid to boost the volume and give special emphasis to certain frequencies in an effort to counteract the deficiencies that they have measured in our ears. But that will seldom precisely match our expectations which will always be very personal.

Now he is explaining some of the features of the instrument. But I am only half listening. Instead I am fascinated by the different qualities of the sounds. He taps a pencil on the glass top of the desk. It causes a kind of double report in my ears. Definitely not natural. I tell him that his voice sounds a bit metallic, a bit edgy, not quite harsh but almost. He clicks the computer mouse on his desk. All sound vanishes. On his PC he has the software that controls the processor in the hearing aid. He clicks the strange boxes and characters on the screen, and abruptly the sound returns. Once more I am in contact. Any better? Can't be sure. I listen to me speaking. I listen to him. But what am I expecting to hear? What was 'normal' before my hearing loss happened? Hard to remember exactly.

Digital hearing aids and the computer programmes that control them are very versatile and wonderfully helpful in the range of options that they offer. Fine tuning can change the whole character of the sounds that I hear. A word like 'digital' can be either warm and normal or harsh and metallic depending on the way the aid is set up. The boosting of some frequencies at the expense of others is rather like mixing colours on a paint palette – yellow can be changed to shades of orange, or blue to green depending on what is added. Different frequencies change the 'colour' of sound but if the mixing is not done skilfully, like paint it produces a result that is 'muddy'.

Hearing for John

This digital flexibility can be both good news and not so good. Good because I can be optimistic he will find a setting that will make my hearing experience so much better. Not so good because my expectations and optimism may be greater than even the best, most expensive instruments can deliver. The biggest cause of my frustration is going to be hearing how much of an improvement can be made and yet discovering that the perfect result can be a fiendishly elusive challenge very often impossible to achieve.

Outside in the real world it is all going to sound very different. I must expect that. But I will get used to it. The more I use the aid the more my brain will adjust to the new sounds that it is receiving. He suggests that I give it a try for a week or so. My appointment card gives me a new time on Tuesday week.

Professional – *Starting gently*

When I fit the hearing aid for the first time their reactions can be either quite emotional when they realise that they will be able to hear their friends and families, or disappointed saying that it's very artificial, it's not what they were expecting, it's not fulfilling the picture they have in their mind of what the hearing aid is going to be doing.

They can remember what their normal hearing used to be like, the voices and the music, and some of them expect the hearing aid to give them that ability back again. My job is to try to get the hearing aid to sound as natural as possible but also, by counselling, to get their expectations to match what the hearing aid can do.

I try to explain that it's very much a learning process for them. The majority of them are going to need two or three appointments for fine tuning over the first six weeks. With some it takes less and with others it can take more. With hearing aids improving all the time it's possible to get them right quicker. These adjustments are all part of the support that is so very important if the full benefits that the modern digital hearing aid offers are to be achieved. This is, if you like, part of the total package.

John – *How is it for me?*

He was right, the real world *is* very different. As soon as I get out into the street it hits me. The diesel knock of the taxi engine, a woman's high heels on the pavement – everything sharp, almost deafening. A huge new deluge of sound all around me. When did I last hear it like this? I turn down the volume. The sound gets less but the sharpness has gone. It's all a bit muffled now. I turn it up again. Is this is how it sounded a few moments ago? Can't tell. I'm beginning to feel confused. Maybe I'll just leave it on the original setting until I get home.

I hear voices. They're behind me. Would I have noticed them without the aid? Not sure. Probably not. Was I taking them for granted before, is that why? Who knows? But whatever the reason they're now much more noticeable. Do I want them? Need them? Is this hearing better than before? Not sure. I hum a tune. The resonance in my head is familiar but the tone of voice that I hear is different. How will it sound to other people? Does it matter?

'Well, I don't know,' I announce to myself very loudly. 'Is it OK? How can I tell? Who cares? What's for lunch?' Then, even louder: 'Hamburger and sushi in a pie? Tum-dee-dum-dee-dum! Testing! Testing! Four nine four five. Nice girls love a nice time.'

My words fight the traffic noise. How do I sound? I badly want to hear someone else speak. Instead, I notice a well-dressed elderly lady leading a tiny designer dog. Both glare at me apprehensively. She makes a protective

Hearing for John

grab for the pooch and throws fearful glances in my direction as she crosses to the other side of the street clearly determined to get out of my way. 'Dum-dee-dum-dee-dum,' I sing to myself experimenting with the volume while I wait for the lights to change. 'Dum-dum, ho-ho. Pigs' trotters. How's your father Arthur? Sick as a parrot, carrot.' Two girls with Starbucks coffees move carefully away from me avoiding eye contact. Everything sounds so different. How loud am I? From the looks I'm getting, quite loud.

At the railway station the loudspeaker booms. It hits my ears. I cannot decode what it is saying. In my seat on the train I have a similar problem with the guard. Whatever he is telling us or asking for is a foreign language. Am I safe to travel like this? What will happen if there is an emergency? Will I know before it is too late? Would I be better without the aid? Mustn't think like this. Not good for my confidence. Like he said it's going to take time. I must be patient allow my brain to learn new ways to decode.

Easy to say but not so easy to handle. I'm feeling almost light-headed. I've been used to something very different. Now I've got a load of new noises that are pulling me in totally new directions. They not only sound different, they make me feel different physically. My whole being seems to have changed. Exaggeration? No, it's not. That's how it feels right now. Sounds go right inside me. And they're very different from what they were an hour ago. Sounds are my life and, if they change, my life changes. I'm not being dramatic or hysterical. I have to face it.

Hearing for John

The rumble of the train at speed is really very loud. I see mouths moving but whatever they are saying is drowned by the wheels on rails and the general creaking and jolting. This is what I have been told to expect: background noise. Except it's not in the background now; it's dominating everything else. My digital miracle is picking up the loudest sounds around me and it is not sorting them as cleverly as my ear and brain would do 'normally'. My brain's filter mechanism was amazingly good at allowing me to focus on what I needed to hear under even the most difficult conditions. I took it for granted.

The problem of background noise will always loom large. The ear and brain working together have an extraordinary ability to pick and mix sounds. Although the hubbub of a party or restaurant, the music in a disco or even the animated conversation of a group of friends can all be hugely noisy – even deafening – the ear allows us to pick up the words of someone we are chatting to, even when there's quite a lot of space between us.

Hearing aids do not have the same ability to discriminate. The bottom line always used to be that the aid would amplify the loudest sound in any environment and that might not be the sound we most wanted to hear. However there has been considerable progress in the digital systems. The mini-computer can now be programmed to analyse the incoming sounds, let through the frequencies that we need most with our special hearing, and damp down the other frequencies that we do not need. Nevertheless the result is seldom going to be perfect. Apart from anything else the aid can only take in so much noise. There is a limit and when sounds exceed it even the most sophisticated aid cannot cope. This produces two big problems for us.

First, a lack of decoding. We find it difficult and often impossible to understand clearly what is being said to us. This tests the tolerance of other people. They simply cannot imagine how difficult not being able to hear can be. They may say they understand but they don't. Yes, they are aware of the noise around them. That's why they are speaking louder. And the louder they speak the louder others speak until the vicious spiral produces a group of individuals who are shouting at each other just to make themselves heard. But that doesn't help us much because the louder they shout the more sound the hearing aid has to absorb with negative results from our point of view.

The second problem for us is stress. The volume and the type of sounds can cause extreme discomfort. It can all be too much. We become tense. The more the noise winds us up the more our stress levels interfere with our ability to decode. We are at our best when we are relaxed. Under pressure our hearing gets noticeably worse. This is something everyone who wears a hearing aid has to cope with. It is, at the present time, unavoidable. So what do we do?

First, we make whatever adjustments we can to the aid itself. Most have a simple volume control. By turning it down we reduce the amount of sound coming into the aid and help to make sure that it doesn't get overloaded. Strangely this will often help us to hear more because other people will be speaking loudly. Some aids have more than one programme. The mini-computer may be set up to switch automatically to a programme that is designed to handle noisy backgrounds or there may be a control that allows us to do this manually. Either way the noise problem can be reduced substantially.

However, there are other times when the babble is just too much. No way to get away from it. No way to decode what people are saying. We don't want them to think we are inattentive or rude. On the other hand we cannot endure the agony for too long.

If this happens to you there is one fail-safe trick you can try. Simply say that your hearing aid has signalled overload. You need to turn if off completely for a short while to allow it to stabilise. Even if they suspect that you are not being completely accurate they will appreciate that you are trying to get yourself out of a difficult situation as diplomatically as possible. Switch the aid off and leave it off while you let your jangling nerves get themselves onto a more even keel. Then after a while when you feel you can face it, switch on again. You will find it a bit easier to handle the noise. Even a short break can make a big difference. Of course you have missed conversation but you wouldn't have heard it well anyway. And the switch-off has helped to reduce the stress. This works for me. However hearing professionals will doubtless have other tactics for you to use.

Professional – *Loud or quiet, it's always there*

The brain naturally filters sounds to give you what you do and don't want to hear. With some of us this filtering system works better than with others. I see people in their twenties and thirties complaining of not hearing because of background noise. But when we do a hearing test their thresholds of different frequencies are within normal limits. Their filtering system is just not as flexible as others.

If you weren't very good at filtering sound when your hearing was normal you won't be with a hearing aid. That's why when I fit hearing aids to some people they can go into different environments and cope with background noise whereas others can't.

John – *My problem, your problem*

When at last I get home I jump at the sound of her voice behind me. It is very different. And there's that big hall effect around everything. 'How is it?' she asks. I see the anxiety in her eyes. This is very important for her. Is it the great leap forward we are hoping for?

'He says it may take a little while,' I tell her. 'Got to get used to it. Like a new pair of shoes.'

'What next?'

'Apparently I may need two or three adjustments to get it right. I have another appointment on Tuesday, week after next.'

She still looks worried. 'Do you think it will work for you, really?' She's not stupid. Of course she cares. For her it is every bit as important as it is for me. It has to be good. Good for me, good for her. So is it? How can I possibly know? It's still too soon, too strange.

How much of this strangeness will I be able to tolerate? If the sound quality is not to my liking there is absolutely nothing I can do about it. And right now there's a whole lot that I reckon needs changing. Can I wait for twelve days? I have to. Don't have a lot of choice, do I? There it is again, the Big Problem: I am not in control. Is this what made my grandfather throw his aid away?

I dial the talking clock inspired by the thought that, at the very least, this should allow me to discover how different the programmes sound. With my earlier analogue aids I didn't have anything like the same choices. The earliest ones had no manual controls.

Hearing for John

Later there was a volume control that I could adjust. Then there was a choice of four separate programmes which allowed the hearing professionals to talk about four hearing aids in one package. Now with this digital system I have five channels each giving a different mix of frequencies. I need to sort out which ones suit me best.

I try them one at a time: channels 1, 2, 3, 4 and the T programme which should be best with the telephone – but I really can't tell if it is. I also try different volumes, louder, softer. 'At the third stroke… Beep! Beep! Beep!' Again. And again. Did anybody think to test the tolerance of a user who has to listen to that mind numbing noise time after time? It's getting on my nerves; but I need to do it. This is serious research.

Suddenly, I realise there are big holes in my methodology. I haven't noted which combinations I have used and how they sounded. Worse still, my index finger has fiddled with the two slide controls on the telephone itself changing the volume and the tone. What a mess!

Calm down. Start again. Paper and pen. The aid has its own beeps to tell me which programme I am using and at what volume. Soon I have three columns showing the results – programme, volume, comment. 'No better.' 'Not this one.' 'Horrible.' 'No good.' There isn't one that seems right. But at least I'm learning what doesn't work. Now what? Should I go through the whole business again, changing the telephone volume and then the tone? Yep, that's what it needs. Except it's impossible. Right now I'm confused, out of patience and that talking clock is sending me round the bend.

Hearing for John

However it's not all wasted. I'm discovering what my digital 'friend' in my ear can do. I am also learning to pay more attention to what I hear.

Sounds are triggers that push my thinking in various directions causing me to do what I do. When, from time to time, new ones intrude – a shout, a squeal of brakes, a dog barking – they catch my attention for just as long as it takes me to decode how important they are at that precise moment so that I can either transfer my focus to them or leave them on one side as a passing memory. Now that my hearing is changing the triggers are less likely to work in quite the same way. As a result I will act and feel differently even with the help of technology. This is why I believe the hearing aid cannot be compared with the mobile phone, the Mp3 player, the PC or any of the other devices in the long list of inventions that have made such huge differences to our lives. It operates in a totally different dimension affecting my emotions in a way no other instrument can. How I am, even who I am, can be changed by the impact the digital aid makes on my consciousness, my moods, even my vitality.

In this scenario the star performer is the audiologist who has the power to change positively (but sometimes not) my connections with my world. How well I hear, in fact how well I cope with life, is largely in the hands of this professional whose experience and expertise can determine how rich and rewarding my hearing experiences will be. Voices and noises can sound warm and sympathetic or harsh and jarring depending on the digital settings.

Hearing for John

And yet, ironically, the judgement on whether they are right for me is entirely in *my* hands! I alone have that absolutely personal experience. Only I can explain and possibly complain about the way sounds are affecting me. It is important for me to be aware how sensitive this judgement can be and, even more crucially, to learn how to communicate it clearly. This is so much more than just a question of technology and digital know-how. My emotions are involved and they are extremely sensitive and vulnerable to variations in the way I perceive the quality of sound that a hearing aid delivers. The remarkable teamwork between my ears and my brain, that from birth has been developing and fine tuning, now has more players – the designers and makers of digital systems, and the hearing professionals who recommend them and adjust them to my uniquely special needs. If this is to be my new 'normality' I get the feeling that the learning curve is going to be steep.

Professional – *New hearing, new learning*

I always try to get people to wear their hearing aid on a regular basis and to tell me about any problems they have with it. There are times when they start by saying that it's sounding pretty horrible but I know that if only they will give it a chance they will probably get used to it.

Settings that the computer shows are right for the hearing aid according to the audiogram quite often don't sound right to the patient. Whether their perception is right or wrong that's the view that they have and that is what I have to work with. I may believe my judgement is right but if the aid doesn't sound right to them they may end up not wearing it so what's the point?

Of course there's a halfway house and it may take a month or two to move them from where they think they want to be to where I think they ought to be. Quite often this works well and they come back after a few weeks and say, 'yes, I've got used to it, you were right to start with'. But it can be a very gradual process.

The brain is very adaptable and if you can give yourself a chance to get used to the hearing aid you will benefit. It may take time and you may have to be patient. In my experience it is really important not to give up. In the end you will find that you get so used to the slightly different kind of hearing that the digital system gives you that you will no longer think of it as being different.

Hearing for John

When people come back for an adjustment I ask them to describe what they are hearing. This really is the crux of it, to get information about their experiences and then to interpret what they're saying by changing the settings of the hearing aid. It's easier with some people than with others. I ask questions but how much I can do to improve the settings to match the very personal ways in which they can hear always partly depends on their answers.

Fine tuning really does rely on a good dialogue that gives me reasonably accurate information. What helps me most is when they remember specific situations – for example: 'I was in this business meeting and I couldn't hear because the room was echoing,' or 'I was in a restaurant and I couldn't hear what the waiter asked me, I could only hear the music.' Or somebody remembers being in a small group of people where they could actually hear people who were further away slightly better than the ones sitting right next to them. Descriptions like that are very useful. I might try compressing louder sounds and louder speech, turning them down a little bit, while turning up quieter speech. Sometimes general descriptions, boomy, basey, metallic, can help me fine tune the general tone and make it more natural.

The hard ones for me are, 'it doesn't sound right', 'it sounds alien', 'artificial'. They don't give a lot of information and they don't really mean much. Some of the manufacturers now supply diaries so that patients can keep notes that describe situations. That gives me something very specific to work with and it can also help them to remember the kind of problems that they experienced at the time.

And then there is data logging. Some hearing aids are designed to store information not only about how much they have been used in what kind of environment but also which programme and what volume has been selected. This can provide a read-out showing, for example, that every time they go into a quiet situation they increase the volume three decibels and when they're in a noisy environment they decrease it by two. With the computer I can change the settings with a couple of clicks so that the next time they go into the quiet they don't have to increase the volume and when they go into noise they don't have to turn the volume down. Data logging can also sometimes be a bit of a giveaway. In one case the patient told me, 'it doesn't sound very nice,' and when I checked the read-out it showed he hadn't been using it at all.

John – *'Flavours' of hearing are subtle: discuss*

Fine tuning a hearing aid is a progressive process. With careful collaboration between the audiologist and me it becomes a very positive and rewarding experience for both of us. On a technical level changing the settings delivers a different mix of frequencies that show on the computer. I may notice a difference or, when the adjustment is very slight, I may not. However there is also an emotional level that I find fascinating although very hard to describe.

Any change in the way I hear seems to affect my self-image. When I notice that normal sounds are suddenly different I lose contact with familiarity and nothing seems quite the same. This has an important effect on how I feel about myself, especially if there's a change in the way my voice sounds to me. You may understand this better if you think how you feel about yourself when your nose and ears are bunged up with a heavy head cold.

Fine tuning my hearing aid can have a similar effect on me. Although the sounds it is receiving may be the same as usual, when adjustments add or take away some of the ingredients (frequencies) I notice that my hearing has a different flavour. *Different from what?* The flavour I had before. *Yes, but what was that?* Difficult to find the right words. I just know there's been a change.

An example from my daily routine may make this clearer. My morning cup of coffee can be reassuring as long as it is made with the usual ingredients. But with less milk or more sugar the flavour is suddenly unfamiliar. Even though the basic coffee itself has not changed the unexpected taste may give me a feeling that is strange, even disturbing. Detected by my sense of taste and smell the cause of this unfamiliar flavour can be easily understood and just as easily remedied.

My hearing works in a different dimension. I feel as though I am floating in a giant bubble that contains my own personal atmosphere. Emotional, intangible and always very personal this comfortably familiar floating sensation is my awareness. Even though I can't describe it as a physical presence I can feel how much it influences my connections with everyone and everything around me. But when the flavour of my hearing is altered the atmosphere in my bubble changes. What I then find difficult is trying to find the right words to explain precisely what is different about this new floating sensation and what it is now doing to my life.

Please remember, these are my very personal thoughts. Yours will be equally personal.

I wonder what he'll say if I tell him I haven't been wearing it all the time? Am I a wimp? Too weak-kneed to take the pressure? It's a wonderful instrument, a fantastic example of digital intelligence in miniature. Someone tells me there's as much computing power in the tiny chip as in some home PCs (however much that is). It's in my ear helping to bring my life back to normal. And it's driving me nuts with all its weird sounds that are like nothing I have ever heard before. No it's not. I'm being hysterical. They're not weird or bizarre or horrible. They're just not right. And I can't

Hearing for John

stand them pouring into my head. When I wear it I feel like I'm on a different planet: too loud, too sharp, and the constant hollow sound behind her voice when she asks me, a hundred times every hour, if it's all right.

He's not surprised when I confess. A little nod suggests that he rather expected it. I tell him it's too loud, too harsh, too different. Again he nods. Takes time to get used to it, he says. After the adjustments everything should stop being quite so strange and difficult. If they're not right he will do more, step by step. He's sure I will find there are improvements. But he stresses again that the instrument can only do part of the work. It cannot correct the way my ear performs. It can only change the strengths of the various sounds that go into my ear to compensate for the ones in which I am weakest.

He makes it all seem so easy. Get used to a completely new kind of hearing experience. Don't worry, everybody has a learning curve. No rush. This isn't a competition. Except I feel that I'm not making much of a contribution.

He asks me to describe what I don't like. My answers are about as sharp as a piece of fudge. This is a very definite communication problem. What am I supposed to say? How do I find the right words? I can't think like he thinks. I don't have his knowledge. Every day of his life he is talking about decibels, frequencies, settings, compression, feedback and all the other bits of techno-speak that are part of his profession. I have half-an-hour of his time and, even though I've been kicking doors with my frustrations, I can't find the simple words to tell him how I feel about the sounds that this little

Hearing for John

instrument is sending into my head. What if I say that the car sounds like gargle? Can he really make sure it sounds to me like it's running on petrol?

The more specific I can be the better. I must attempt some way of explaining that background noise is drowning everything; echoing restaurants are specially bad; I can hear male voices that are deep much better than females; it's hard to hear people at meetings; impossible to decode comments in a car; I can no longer enjoy a solo violin playing with a big orchestra because I can't hear the high notes. I need to say how sounds are making me feel emotionally – warm, irritated, frustrated, dizzy – and why I think they're making me feel this way – too sharp, too hollow, too distant.

But then very quickly I begin to discover that the way I describe something will mean one thing to me and something different him so it pays to keep my comments as simple as possible almost as though I am trying to explain to someone who doesn't speak my language very well – which of course is right. He has his own ideas and I have mine and it is too much to hope that we will think alike in any meaningful way. If we do that is magic but who believes in magic?

How much easier it would be if I could be offered a list of simple yes or no choices to indicate what works for me and what doesn't. But that seems impossible because I'm hearing a whole range of sounds that come together in one total experience and I haven't any idea which of them is giving everything this flavour that is unlike anything I have been used to.

This is where the difference between treating hearing and eyesight is possibly most noticeable.

Measuring any loss of eyesight is comparatively routine. With very well-established tests for short-sight, long-sight, sensitivity to glare, etc, within half-an-hour an optometrist has an accurate picture of how each of our eyes is performing and what strength and type of lenses will correct the loss. The prescription is very precise and once we have our new glasses the amount of after care that we may need is likely to be considerably less than with our hearing.

He tells me to take my time. He doesn't mind if I'm fumbling for words. But I mind, very much. I feel so guilty (yes, there it is again!). So inadequate, so powerless to achieve any real progress. Seems to me there is a powerful need to build a more precise kind of bridge between us. In amongst the excitements of digital wizardry has anyone thought about a simple way for me to share my feelings with him so that he will understand precisely?

Maybe we need a completely new kind of digital phonetic 'dictionary' so that we can establish benchmarks that leave no room for misunderstandings. We learned something similar as tiny children when we were taught to associate pictures and actions with simple sounds. Perhaps a computer programme can be linked to a simple game that lets us select visual images that we most closely associate with sounds that we hear using the hearing aid. This will give a profile that can be compared against a profile of images associated with 'normal' hearing. It should then be a simple matter to fine tune the settings of the hearing aid to compensate for the differences.

Hearing for John

He makes adjustments. I detect a change but what is it? The quality of his voice is slightly different. Is this because the whole atmosphere has become hollow? No. Perhaps the opposite. Maybe some of the sharpness has gone. A bit muted? I realise that I am feeling, not thinking about this. But I'm not sure which way the atmosphere in my bubble has changed. When he taps the paperknife on the desktop there is no longer a double 'report'. That could mean that there is less sharpness. We try the telephone talking clock – here we go again! The voice and the beeps are not quite as harsh as they were at home. He tells me he has altered the volume for loud and quiet noises. Can I detect it? Can't be sure but he explains that I will do when I get out into the real world. Street noises, background of any kind, always a problem, should be easier.

We stand on the pavement exposed to the full blast of a busy London morning. He speaks to me and I try to judge how well I am hearing him. In my eagerness to clutch at straws I tell him it is better. In what way? How can I tell? I'm just praying that with the work he has done it *will* be better even if at that precise moment I can't say exactly how. Like he says, I have to get used to it.

We go back inside. If I'm really honest I still feel confused. It is impossible for me to understand just how much my reactions to the sounds I am hearing now have changed and in what ways. He puts the settings back to where they were so that I can compare. But this doesn't work for me because my brain has had a sample of the new setting. I have very quickly learned a new pattern of decoding and I cannot wipe out that memory entirely.

Hearing for John

So when I hear the older setting the flavour of the new one lingers in my memory. This is what is confusing. There is nothing to get hold of. Impossible to say a simple 'yes' or 'no'.

Once again I am finding it so hard to communicate in a way that will help him to help me. How do I describe this floating, never mind how it has changed? If I can't get through to him it's my fault – isn't it? Doesn't make me feel very good. It's all so very personal. I feel that in some ways I have to expose whole bits of my life so that he can understand how I hear. I talk about classical music that I enjoy. Sadly he is not a great fan of Mozart or Gershwin so when I explain how my enjoyment of certain pieces has changed, there is no common ground between us. No point telling him how much I miss the high notes in Bruch's violin concerto. Not his taste in music.

Come to think of it our tastes in food are one way of looking at the flavour of sounds that we hear. A chef may prepare a casserole to serve six people. Everyone will be eating the same combination of ingredients and flavours. And yet we will all have different reactions because our ideas about food are unique to each of us. The chef can only know about our tastes from what we tell him: we like it spicy but not too much (what's too much?) we don't like the smell of garlic, we prefer meat without sauces added, etc.

For my digital hearing casserole the ingredients are combinations of frequencies set at different volumes using the programmes designed by the makers of the aid. Although the recipe suggested by the audiogram and interpreted by the audiologist and the computer may be digitally right for me my personal tastes may make it very difficult for me to enjoy the flavour of the sound. To which the hearing aid industry will respond by saying that I have simply got to learn to accept the new flavours in the same way as I learned to like the original ones that are no longer possible for me.

Like it or lump it? Not really. Yet there simply cannot be unlimited time or tolerance for my strictly personal problems. I need to be grateful that I can be helped in any way at all and, believe me, I am. But it is still very frustrating, because I am convinced that there is so much more that the technology can achieve on a bespoke basis if only there could be a more precise way of describing what I am hearing and what I think I am missing.

Throughout thirty years this has always been a problem for me. For all that the audiologists and I seem to have managed quite well. It has been a team effort. They ask perceptive questions and then make allowances for the kind of answers I give. Difficult for them when you think about the wide range of patients they treat. Age, education and life experiences prompt all kinds of contrasting comments that describe very individual flavours of hearing.

My own solutions have come from trying to make sure I notice *how* I am hearing on a daily basis. I try to make a mental note of where I am, what is going on, and how much I feel that my decoding is affected. When I use the volume control and the programme selector switch I also do my best to remember how well the changes work. I guess it would be even better to have a diary but, being realistic, I know I would find it hard to keep it up-to-date. In any event my memory serves me reasonably well because my hearing is an ongoing obsession for me.

We all live in a bubble of awareness. Usually we don't notice. It is just there all the time. It is what we are. With my hearing loss my awareness is different now from what it was when I could hear normally. I do notice but not very often. Most of the time I can accept what it is and take it for granted. This works very well as long as nothing changes it. Fine-tuning does. And for a short while afterwards I am very conscious of a different flavour of hearing. Quite soon, however, my brain adjusts and the new flavour becomes a comfortable and normal background.

Tricia – *Some choice!!*

'Whaddya wannabe?' snarled the Bad Fairy, brandishing her wand, 'blind or deaf?' Tricky question.

Not so long ago, there was a saying: 'Men never make passes at girls wearing glasses' and any child needing to wear spectacles was likely to be taunted as 'four eyes' in the school playground. Nowadays spectacles have become a fashion accessory. Sunglasses are worn whether the sun shines or not. Designer frames cost hundreds of pounds. People buy glasses to match their outfits. And if you don't like the idea of being hemmed in by frames there is a bewildering array of contact lenses on offer – or you may try laser surgery.

Many years ago I met a prominent personality who was deaf. He wore one of those old-fashioned earpieces connected with a very obvious white wire to a large box in his breast pocket. He explained that he wanted to make sure everyone he met understood he was deaf.

As far as I can see, this is in complete contrast to the hearing aid industry. Their advertising emphasises how small and invisible all the latest digital devices have become. If you have a hearing loss, nobody who meets you needs to know – 'hidden hearing', 'micro technology', 'normal life', and so on. They even suggest you hide your hearing aid in the frame of clear lens glasses, for heaven's sake. People should think you are going blind, rather than deaf! So if you have sight problems you happily advertise; hearing problems you hide.

Hearing for John

It's as if the perception of hearing loss is stuck in the days of the bath chair, the ear trumpet, and Great Aunt Florrie, who you dreaded because she got cross when she couldn't hear even if you shouted. She and that army friend of your father's, who was absolutely fearsome because he was always telling you to speak up, epitomised what deaf people are all about. Perhaps that thinking may be changing (it certainly needs to) but there is no doubt that at present if you say you are deaf or hard of hearing all the old images instantly spring to mind.

Ironically growing numbers of (mostly) young people these days go around with wires or strange-shaped, brightly coloured objects dangling from their ears. Mp3 players, mobile phones – all the cool people have them. How odd that many of them may need hearing aids before they are very much older simply because the excessive noise they are subjecting their ears to now will be the cause of hearing problems in the future.

John – *Ignorance or indifference?*

When we think about public awareness and support for other disabilities it seems that hearing loss has a lot of ground to make up.

Wheelchair access is perhaps one of the most noticeable examples, now so common that we take it for granted not only in public places but also in many privately owned facilities. It cannot be otherwise. The law commands it. And then there are the neat signs that tell us about the availability of toilet facilities and parking spaces for the disabled. Road junctions and pedestrian crossings have sounds and pavement surfaces to help anyone with loss of eyesight. All these show a steadily growing acknowledgement that many of us have special needs.

Promoting general awareness of physical disability must surely be helpful for the dignity and self-respect of people who want to handle their handicaps positively, and rightly so. In harsher times crutches, walking sticks and wheelchairs would have usually produced, at best, a sympathetic but resigned shrug from decision-making shoulders unable to imagine how they could help to ease the weight of disablement other than to donate a few extra quid to the appropriate charity. Towards most of the more obvious disabilities attitudes have greatly improved and, with them, very tangible methods of support. With hearing loss noticeable public awareness has been much slower coming through. Where, for those of us who do not enjoy normal hearing, are the clearly marked public equivalents of wheelchair ramps and handrails and disabled parking spaces?

Induction loops are becoming more common but their presence and the ways in which they are operated don't, in anything like the same way, imprint themselves on the minds of people who have no need to use them. And when they *are* installed how much priority is given to making sure that they are actually operating properly? Do proprietors and their staff have any clear idea how much someone with hearing loss can benefit from using the T programme? And how well have they understood that, by helping to avoid the inevitable confusions hearing loss can cause not only for those of us who are hard of hearing but also for the people with whom we are in contact, a department store or railway booking office will save time and improve their own efficiency?

For those of us who can benefit it is frustrating to find that a loop system isn't working (although we may be tempted to wonder whether it is indeed the system that is at fault or our hearing aid). RNID receives letters which complain of supermarkets where, although the presence of a system is shown with a notice at the cash tills, staff have said that they don't know how it operates and in one case confessed that they didn't even know what it is for. Ignorance or indifference? Ignorance on the part of staff may be understandable but on the part of the management, who are responsible for training them, we can only hope that only lack of direct exposure to deaf and hard of hearing customers is the real reason behind what appears to be indifference.

Hearing for John

If there is lack of general awareness perhaps a good part of the responsibility lies with those of us who, despite our difficulties, are reluctant to draw attention to them much less make a fuss. The more we try to be normal the less others see any need for us to be given any special treatment.

One remedy is in our hands. Each one of us can make a positive difference by being more open and proactive in promoting the special needs of hearing disability. The ball is in our court. But unless we play a more determined game we will continue to be losers on the sidelines instead of winning goodwill and practical support. It does absolutely no good to feel embarrassed and over-protective about our hearing loss. The longer we hide it the more we allow others the convenient excuse of believing that the problem is of no great consequence and can be treated as a second or third line priority.

At the same time makers of support systems could also play a bigger part. With induction loops more could be done to make them obvious in public places. Indicator lights together with notices conspicuously announcing: 'Hearing aid induction loop ON' (or something similar) would not only reassure the wearers of hearing aids but would also alert staff to the operational status of the system. Equally important the existence of the loop would be automatically brought to the notice of the public and with it an awareness of the reason for its existence.

There are however encouraging signs of progress much of it prompted by the Disability Discrimination Act which requires anyone offering services to the public, including churches and schools, to make provision for people with hearing problems. For example when a classroom is wired with a loop system (many of which are very portable and inexpensive) a teacher can use an easily worn microphone to communicate clearly with any pupil using a hearing aid switched to T. Railways and underground stations have for some years had emergency points where anyone needing assistance can press a panic button and ask for help. I would normally have ignored the facility, knowing that against the background noise it would be impossible for me to hear the inevitable questions that the remote helper would ask. However at our local suburban railway station, I was encouraged to see the familiar ear sign beneath the help point indicating the presence of an induction loop. This is one more big step in the right direction. Did I try it out? No. Does it work? I certainly hope so.

Tricia – *Badges of pride?*

I have always been fascinated by the way ants scurry. They form long, busy lines with an occasional individual going in the opposite direction against the flow. As it passes, this solitary ant will pause from time to time in front of one of the others in the procession. Is this for some kind of greeting or exchange of information?

Seen from a high building people on a busy street behave in a similar way. They appear to touch base momentarily and move on. Yet even the briefest contacts help to keep us together. We need them to make us feel that we belong. We try to connect and we hope for a response. It's a two-way exchange, all too easily upset when one part doesn't work.

John is always quick to react to friends and colleagues – provided he hears them. But, 'Hi John!' usually won't register with him if the speaker is not in his line of sight. There is a pause while everyone waits for John to answer and when he doesn't there may be a momentary hesitation or flash of irritation and then life continues. The greeting is seldom repeated and John has missed the chance of a contact that I know he would have enjoyed. He looks normal acts normally and, because there is no outward sign of any problem, people expect normal behaviour from him.

This means he is expected to respond sensibly even if they talk behind his back or say something important when the coffee machine is noisily frothing milk for cappuccino. The fact that he can hear some things sometimes only makes matters worse. People either

Hearing for John

don't know, forget or can't be bothered to remember that John's hearing needs special treatment. Ironically it's the success with which he conceals the problem that causes most of the difficulties.

It's always going to be a bit of a conundrum. No-one would expect him to join in a game of football if he was leaning heavily on a pair of crutches. Nobody would be unfeeling enough to ask him to share their view of a beautiful painting if he was wearing opaque dark glasses and holding a white cane. People usually behave with sympathy and understanding towards disablement if they know about it. Which is the problem with hearing.

Should he wear some kind of a badge that would make it hard for him to enjoy the near normality that I know he wants to have; or should he continue to risk the frustrations that his occasional lapses cause for him and for others? I suspect that the second option is his preference but I rather wish it could be easier to find a reasonable solution somewhere between the two.

All this came into particularly sharp focus one morning at the supermarket. Seated at one of the checkout desks was a young woman with a sign prominently fixed to her blouse. The bold lettering read: 'I am deaf. Please speak slowly and clearly. I will be happy to help you.' The reaction from customers was friendly. Almost without exception they spoke to her in way that without the badge they would probably not have done. To me this was a wonderful example of how most of us are quite willing to provide whatever support we can when we can see that someone is disabled and all the more so when it is obvious that they are doing everything they

Hearing for John

can to help themselves. Perhaps what the check-out girl did is the kind of common sense action that is needed to make everyone more aware of the problems that are caused by hearing loss and how being positive can go a long way towards helping to overcome them.

Hearing Concern now offers a number of tastefully designed badges which John can wear. One of them, based around a line drawing of a bear, says: 'Bear with me. I am hard of hearing.' The others all offer an equally simple message. The more they appear on shirt fronts and lapels the more they will help to show that our problem is widely shared which will have an increasing effect on public awareness. Will John wear them? That will always be very much personal choice.

Incidentally, do ants 'speak' or do they make meaningful contact though some kind of special telepathy? They have eyes but apparently their main form of communication is through smell. No mention of sound. Nevertheless it is clear from their body language that connecting is a critical part of their existence – just as it is with us.

John – *Brainpower on my side*

Learn to adapt? Come to terms with the problems? Can I do it? If I can what's at the end of the game? 'Normal' hearing? No, never again. Not possible. See? I'm learning already. I can compromise like anyone else. What can I look forward to? Hard to believe but I *will* get used to it. I'm learning to trust him.

On the way home the trains sound a bit different. Better? If quieter is better then they sound better. The new volume settings have clicked in and I don't feel the harshness in the underground and at Waterloo. The announcements inside the carriage on the Bakerloo tube seem to be clearer. I keep hearing 'Elephant and Castle'. Do I hear all of it or just enough for my memory to fill in the gaps? Hard to tell. Perhaps this doesn't matter. If I get the meaning surely that's all that counts? I hear 'Charing Cross' and, depending on the speed of the train, 'the next station is…'. I even hear a word or two in the chatter between the two women sitting opposite. Would I hear them without the hearing aid? I'm afraid to take it off to try.

When I get home she is at the computer. Can't see her face but I hear her speak. So I guess she wants to know about my day. 'Could be worse,' I tell her. 'I can live with it.'

She turns to face me, slightly irritated. 'That's not very nice.' Then it dawns. 'Didn't hear me did you? I said Jeanie's running late. She won't be here for about an hour.'

Hearing for John

Whoops! Doesn't help that she knows Jeanie isn't my idea of fun. Her face relaxes. She knows that as usual I didn't decode. 'So,' she asks, 'has he made any difference?'

What do I say? She is hoping for a big smile and, 'Fantastic! It's all going to be OK.' No chance. Truth is he *has* made a difference but it doesn't seem to be helping very much. That's not what she wants to hear. And I don't want to say it. So negative. Wimpish.

'Too soon to know,' I tell her. 'Ask me again in a couple of days.' By then I am supposed to have taken on board all the new sounds and worked out how to adapt to them. Will that be long enough? Can I relearn a lifetime in two days?

'Will it be better by next week?' She's thinking about the long weekend with our friends. Are we going to have a replay of the problems we had last time or will this be different? Again I feel guilty. We are a great team and we've had some really good times together. But will it be tough going for all of us because of me?

'You know I want it to be better,' I tell her. Has she any idea how much I want this?

'Will you see him again before we go to them?'

'No space in his diary.' I see her disappointment. 'Anyway he thinks it will be better for me to give these new settings a good try before he makes any more changes. He has asked me to keep notes of what happens.'

On the way home I had noticed some sounds that I am sure he could easily change if only I could get back to him right now. But that's not on. Why can't I have

Hearing for John

a little control box to make my own adjustments? That would solve everything.

I'm conscious of a presence behind me. Younger daughter is there with a face perplexed and in her hand some papers that look like a job application. She must have said something but in my reverie I missed it.

'She's asking you,' her mother explains patiently, 'if you have a few moments to help her?' My daughter's eyes cloud. My face has given the wrong answer not because I don't want to help but because I am inwardly upset by my failure to hear her question the first time. 'Of course if you don't have time…'

No problem whatever it takes; it's always fun to get involved with her work. But not for the first time I realise that the stress of my day, struggling to deal with the new settings, has given my face a forbidding mask that is sending totally the wrong signals. Both she and her mother have misunderstood. Whatever I say now has to overcome the negative feelings I have generated without meaning to, which makes me feel bad. My grim face is a problem. It seems to have become a bit of a fixture. Worse still I don't know it is happening. What else is changing in my behaviour? If I don't know I can't put it right. Without doubt I have a lot more to learn than simply getting used to new sounds. And this is where I have to confront my own personal attitude.

When I can't hear what is said I may direct some of my negative feelings towards people who are involved. Why can't they talk more slowly, more clearly? Why doesn't the person at the call centre speak directly into the headset microphone? Why won't the shop assistant look at me so I can hear what she is saying? And,

Hearing for John

underneath it all, there is a growing feeling against myself. I start to be self-conscious, self-critical and stressed. All of these work against me when instead I should be trying to remain confident and relaxed. That's difficult.

My negatives are understandable. But they just make matters worse. If I am stressed when I am trying to hear and if I am more aware of my hearing loss than the words people are saying I am up against a double whammy. Physical tension can affect the muscles in my jaw and neck which can in turn affect my ear canal reducing the amount of space for sounds to get through to my inner ear.

However, it need not be like that. If I can relax and trust my brain's flexibility I will find that it will quite quickly adjust to the different qualities and volumes of sound that my ears are detecting. It works in its own time. As that learning curve becomes more developed my earlier memories of sounds are replaced with new ones.

These new decodes form the basis of our reorganised personal hearing world. If we value them and value our own achievements in adapting we can treat them as a new normality. We have grown up thinking we need to be like other people, at least, and better than them if possible. When we find that our changed hearing makes it difficult to deal with them in their terms we may experience doubts about ourselves. But that's negative thinking. A better way is to value our own world and our changed hearing more highly. We need to build up an attitude that is not afraid to be different and owes nothing to anyone in terms of confidence and personal dignity.

Part of the secret is to not regret the passing of the older decodes but instead rise to the challenge of learning this new 'music' of sounds that has been caused by our changed hearing. More than a challenge we may choose to think of this as an adventure helping us to discover new confidence and self-respect.

Tricia – *Getting on his good side*

In many ways we have all had to learn to adapt. And increasingly we find that we are not the only ones. For example, at a recent wedding when we joined other guests at the table indicated by the seating plan John asked if he could change places with someone in order to favour his good ear. That started it. The whole table instantly degenerated into a musical chairs farce as most of them had a hearing problem and therefore a good side.

Now it seems to happen all the time. Forget about polite convention. Placing the most important lady guest on the host's right is almost certainly not on. The new game is that before you sit down everyone points out their best ear and then hopefully matches it up with somebody else's best ear. Alternatively, choose who you most want to chat with and make sure you sit next to them. Never mind if this leads to a row of males facing a row of females like a barn dance.

Most important of all I must never sit beside John's good ear (unless there are only the two of us, when this is allowed). Preferably I must sit as far away from him as possible otherwise important comments from our friends will be drowned by my voice. Not surprising really. I've had to develop a specially emphatic way of speaking just to make sure that we have the best chance of avoiding all those little misunderstandings that happen when he thinks what I've said is quite different from what I really did say.

Hearing for John

What I've also learned is that John finds it hard to change gear between voices that are loud and others that are quieter when they are all competing for space at the same time in the same place. He accepts that a jolly chat between old friends can sound very excited with loud bursts of hilarity. But if he's not directly in the firing line, and not actively engaged in that particular golden moment of delight, the constant volume of noise from the happy voices will have him fighting to understand what is being said more quietly by somebody sitting right beside him.

This is why, if we are entertaining just one other couple in our home and the wife is one of my good friends, John's ideal solution would be to have the females in one room and the males in another. From long experience I have found that, however quietly we two females think we are murmuring our gossip, at the end of the evening I am told that it was impossible for John to hear Nick or Leo because we were shouting at the tops of our voices. Makes me realise how well my hearing copes with the extremes of sound and how much I take it for granted.

John – *Most valuable of my valuables*

I played against him in the first set. Like the rest of us seniors he has worked out cunning ways of covering the court with minimum effort – age and agility and the winning score were definitely on his side. What's more, he and his tennis partner were clearly communicating very well with quietly muttered tactical planning between points.

It was only while we were waiting to play together in the next game that I noticed the ear mould and the tubing to the aid behind his right ear.

'What make is it?' I ask quietly.

'Don't know. It's digital. NHS.'

'You manage very well,' I tell him. I feel quite envious. He is always in the thick of social chatting even in the noisy ambiance of the club restaurant where for me conversation is almost impossible because of the loud background of the other voices.

He frowns. 'Can't hear anything this side.' He fingers his left ear. 'Not a thing. Waste of time. Doesn't work.' There's no sign of another aid.

'They fitted you with two?'

He nods. 'Every time I put that one in it makes a terrible noise. Everything is just distorted. Useless.' He shrugs again. 'Got used to no hearing in there. Just means I need to keep people in front of me or on my right side.'

Hearing for John

Join the club, I think. All the games of musical chairs that we play to make the best of our little problems are getting to be so common. It's almost a surprise to find someone that doesn't have a 'good side'. And yet he deliberately chooses to play on the right side of the court which puts his partner and most of the play on his left, his deaf side. It may be because he is only conscious of which side is good and not so good when he is preparing to have a conversation. I wonder if he realises how well he is doing on the tennis court? Clearly the game is keeping his mind off any doubts about his hearing.

'Tried going privately,' he continues, 'but they told me they couldn't do anything for me. Their in-the-ear aids weren't powerful enough. They told me to go NHS.' He probably tried one of those widely-advertised discreet, almost invisible aids that would transform his life and no-one need know. Apparently they work quite well with a mild hearing loss. He doesn't mention cost but money may have also been important.

'Do you have different programmes in your aids?' I ask.

He shakes his head. 'Only the T position. And that doesn't work. Useless.' He's not complaining, just stating a fact with a slight note of annoyance. 'Tried it in the cinemas dozens of times. Never works.'

Same old story. He's right. I have had the same thing even with my top-of-the range aids from two of the most respected makers. 'More than likely,' I tell him, 'the cinema loop system just isn't switched on.'

'Don't go to movies any more,' he says. 'Can't hear a thing.'

'I know the feeling. Neither do I. Subtitles on TV?'

'Couldn't do without them. They're really good with movies on DVD.'

'How about telephones?' I ask.

He grins. 'Just take it out. Can't hear with it in.' Again I am envious. He's quite fortunate. If he can hear telephone voices without the help of a hearing aid the loss in his good ear is clearly not very severe which explains a lot about how confidently he still socialises. But it doesn't solve the problem of zero hearing in his left side.

'Presumably you've told them about your left ear?'

He shakes his head. 'Haven't seen them since the fitting. Always the same with computers. Some things work brilliantly, but others…'

'There's a lot they can do by adjusting the settings,' I tell him confidently.

'Need to,' he answers with feeling. 'Left one's no good at all and something tells me the right one, my good one, could be a whole lot better.'

'You need to get back to your audiologist asap.'

He nods slowly and there is a faraway look in his eye as he fingers his racquet. 'On the day they fitted them they gave me an appointment for the adjustments. Would you believe one year and one day after fitting?'

'Hearing aids can be difficult can't they?' one of the other players observes sympathetically. 'Some of my friends who have them say everything sounds very harsh. Supposed to be better but quite often they make things worse.'

Hearing for John

Why so many negative stories? Of course with anything medical, and not only hearing, we expect to talk about problems. Good news isn't nearly so interesting. But with hearing aids it really doesn't have to be like this. There are so many encouraging improvements and they are becoming more and more frequent. My consultant was right: I have been lucky. The technology and the treatments have more than kept pace with my losses.

'They needn't be harsh or difficult,' I tell her confidently. 'The digital programmes can be adjusted quite easily. We just need to be able to tell the audiologist when it's not working for us.' Sounds good. But is that what really happens, always?

If a mobile phone or a laptop or an Mp3 player isn't giving satisfaction we take it straight back to the shop. And yet with hearing aids many of us who should do just that, don't. Why not? There's usually a guarantee. Are we so frightened off by the mystique of medical jargon that surrounds hearing problems that we don't feel strong enough to make a fuss? Or is it that we have not been told how flexible the systems are and don't have any idea how much can be done? Or do we assume that the professionals know best and we have no option except to get used to the sounds they give us even if they don't seem to be right? In which case the end game is sadly all too predictable: if it makes life too uncomfortable for us, like my grandfather we may simply give up and another sad story will be added to the list. Or is it simply a question of not being able to get to see a hearing professional promptly? This may sometimes happen when audiologists are under pressure and hearing appointments have to be spaced widely apart.

For many people (including some with hearing loss) a hearing aid is just another invention that has to be treated in a purely technical way – which is probably why the work of hearing professionals is not more widely understood and appreciated. Personally, I have always been keenly aware that my hearing aid has a uniquely intimate impact on me in no way similar to any other digital device. And it seems I have been extremely fortunate. All my audiologists and dispensers have been very accessible and astonishingly patient. Yes, it has very often been a matter of trial and error. Yet, in the end the adjustments have yielded good results that have made a huge difference to my ability to connect and live a near normal life.

So I have mixed feelings when I read in a national newspaper a very prominent half page advertisement about a wide range of digital hearing aids being offered at big discounts. Feels to me about as personal and sensitive as cameras and mobiles marked with sale prices stacked on a market stall. The promises are ambitious to say the least. I quote one of them:

'You will be able to hear how speech – or music – **or whichever sounds you want to hear** become crystal clear, **even in noisy surroundings**'.

This is a remarkable claim because it makes no reference to the most important question – what kind of hearing loss do I have? From the hype, I might reasonably expect that my whole hearing experience will be miraculously improved whatever problems I have. Is it fair to raise my expectations in this way?

Of course it can be argued that selling low-cost hearing aids is a public service but in my view it's an empty offer unless it clearly addresses the realities of individual needs and promises unstinting after-care.

Ideally the supply of hearing aids should always be treated with sensitivity and understanding. After-care, which looks after my relationship with the hearing aid, is more important than after-sales service which keeps the system working. Where this is not a big part of the sales pitch perhaps we should wonder why.

However I believe that some of the reasons for the impersonal 'technical' point of view can be traced to our own attitudes. For example:

1. Those of us with hearing problems don't make the effort to explain clearly and energetically enough our feelings about the technology and the support we are being offered. For some reason we don't believe that we have the same claims to sympathy as people with other disabilities. We don't push our case, usually because we have an underlying sense that in some way we are to blame. (We're not!)
2. As with all things medical we submit to the opinions and control of professionals and seldom see any chance of successfully fighting our own corner against their expertise. And while, understandably, we'd hesitate to challenge the prognoses of the physician and surgeon we apply the exactly same caution to the professionals who supply our digital devices. Perhaps this needs a rethink?
3. We are given quality levels and timescales that are set by suppliers. And because we are vulnerable we gladly take what we can get and believe nothing

Hearing for John

more can be done. With more competition in the market place – witness the altered profiles of high street opticians – this may change.

4. We have no way of judging whether the product is working as well as it should and no benchmarks to measure value for money in the way we can with so many other products. So when the aid doesn't give us the sounds that we can live with we have no ammunition with which to fight for a better result. Shouldn't we be trying to change this?

Since the advent of digital systems all my hearing aids have had price tags well into four figures and I have learned to accept that this privately bought, high quality 'total package' will always come at an unavoidably high cost. Bespoke personal treatment from hearing professionals has, for many of us, been the norm. Yet now newspaper advertisements are telling me that digital hearing aids can be mine for a great deal less than 50% of prices I have been accustomed to. How am I to judge which of these is real value for money?

When a good friend retired she decided to try NHS because her expensive digital hearing aids, bought privately, had not been very satisfactory. During the assessment consultation she told the NHS audiologist that she could actually afford to continue buying privately and felt quite guilty about 'wasting public money' on a hearing aid that might go to a more deserving NHS patient. She was astonished when the audiologist quietly put her mind at rest by explaining that NHS buying power had secured remarkable terms from one of the world's leading makers of hearing aids so the actual cost of her aids to NHS would be no more

Hearing for John

than about £170 each and would therefore not make a serious hole in the public purse. Her severe hearing loss (70%) is certainly comparable with mine which means that the aids prescribed for her would most likely have been on a par with top of the range devices prescribed privately for me and for which I paid well in excess of £2,000 each in 2005/6.

Even allowing for any possible misunderstanding this story points to the very considerable price disparities that appear to exist and should prompt us to question whether it is time for there to be a much more open debate about how much hearing aids should cost and why. Incidentally my friend is much happier with her 'free' hearing aids that seem to have cost the NHS little more than one tenth of the price paid for the ones she bought privately.

My own experiences with a digital NHS hearing aid have been less satisfactory. Perhaps hearing losses like mine need special treatment not easily accessible with all the other huge pressures on NHS resources.

It is well established that there are many people with mild hearing loss whose problems can be solved relatively easily. For them low cost high street marketing and servicing of hearing aids should provide a much-needed benefit. Here again there are parallels in changed profiles of prices and services now offered by opticians some of whom are already following a similar route with hearing aids. Yet because of the very individual requirements of people with hearing loss the attraction of lower prices needs to be partnered by sensitive personal service.

Hearing for John

A brief trawl through the internet shows how much things have already started to change. One UK website offers a nationwide service of home visits from fully qualified hearing aid audiologists who can supply leading brand digital hearing aids at discount prices with 'a free and full aftercare programme'.

This kind of offer is promising especially if it helps to get away from the view that a hearing aid is really nothing more than just another clever digital device and, instead, leads to a clearer and more open understanding of the very intimate role it plays in our lives.

Underlying all these thoughts there is a very clear bottom line. Any hearing, no matter how imperfect, will always be better than none. And light years better than the crude enhancement – if indeed there was any at all – that my great-great-grandfather would have struggled to 'enjoy' with the most up-to-date, state-of-the-art ear trumpet!

Tricia – *Moments that make you smile*

The way strangers react to John's deafness can be amusing and, sometimes, over the top. The other day we were in a Spanish supermarket. John, as usual, went to buy the bread but this time he decided that instead of pointing at what he wanted he would like to ask for it. What Spanish words should he use?

'We have pan integral,' I said.

'Pan what?'

'In – te – gral.' The supermarket was noisy and it took several tries on my part, getting steadily louder, before he got it and went off to join the queue.

Nearby a German woman had been watching our interchange with growing amusement. 'That vas zo funny,' she said to me as I passed her.

'Oh, it's just that my husband's deaf,' I replied cheerfully.

Her face fell and she looked really upset. 'I am zo zorry. It seemed like a choke.'

I laughed. 'Really, don't worry. We often joke about it too.' We smiled at each other and went our separate ways. I hope I had reassured her.

On another occasion we were on an excursion. Several coach loads, consisting mostly of older American tourists, had crowded into the small but obligatory gift shop. John was finding the combination of noise, too many people, and indecision at the cash desk a bit much. This was partly due to being deaf and partly to his usual impatience. Onto his face came the expression that causes small children to run howling behind their mothers' skirts and grown men to growl defensively. The full force of this gaze happened to rest upon a lady American tourist who was made of sterner stuff.

'Why is that man looking at me like that?' she demanded of nobody in particular.

I decided to speak up before he was done for harassment. 'He's not looking at you,' I explained. 'He's deaf and the noise in here is too much for him.'

She disintegrated. 'Oh my Gawd, I am SO SORRY. Oh really! I am SO SORRY. I really am SO SORRY.' Her hands went to her face which had turned bright red at what she now perceived to be her crass insensitivity.

'It's okay,' I said gently even though for her it clearly wasn't. But I couldn't think of a way to tell her that John would really have appreciated her concern and her kind apology.

John – *Keywords to open my ears*

Making the best of partial hearing relies quite a lot on inspired guesswork. For my guesses to hit their mark accurately with reasonable frequency it is crucial for me to have some foreknowledge, no matter how hazy, of what the connection is likely to be about.

This is especially true of the way I use the telephone. (We do have an answering machine but I cannot decode the messages.) Caution at all costs is my motto. If I think that the other half of the connection is going to be someone I know well and, even better, someone who I can trust to be patient with my inevitable nonsense I will risk it. But if I have the slightest suspicion that the caller is a stranger I will ignore even the most persistent ringtone.

How do I know which is which? I have a simple system. I let the phone ring. Then I check to see if I recognise the number. If it's familiar and friendly, I ring back. Unfamiliar numbers are ignored, except in very special circumstances – like one memorable April night.

The first try was at about 9.15, late enough to be social rather than business. No message and I didn't recognise the number. Two minutes later the same caller tried again. Once again I let it ring. After the third attempt curiosity got the better of my usual caution. What if it was some kind of emergency, a cry for help? I returned the call.

Hearing for John

Me:	*'Have you just been calling this number 0210 763 890?'*
Mystery caller:	*'Aarrwould, amfilly.' The voice explains helpfully.*
Me:	*'Who are you?'*
Mystery caller:	*'Packikk.' Pause. 'Packikk. Amberaara.'*
Me:	*'I'm sorry. I really don't understand. Who are you?'*
Mystery caller:	*'Weeney orra dress.'*
Me:	*'Who are you? I have a hearing problem.'*
Mystery caller:	*'Offaartie eemee ale.'*

I have a sudden flash of decoding inspiration.

Me (relieved):	*'Yes please. Send me an email.'*
Mystery caller:	*'Moorsyoora dress.'*
Me:	*'My email address…?'*
Mystery Caller:	*'Weewonsenyoo.' suddenly clearer, 'ammat… A mat.'*

I think: 'Is this some kind of promotion?'

Me:	*'I haven't ordered a mat.'*

Abrupt change at the other end.
A female voice now, thankfully familiar.

She:	*'John. We want to send you a map for Tuesday.'*

Hearing for John

My poor good friends. I know them both very well. Face-to-face he has a very cultured, well modulated voice but for my ears the phone turned his words into a kind of audio porridge devoid of any recognisable shape or meaning. Hers was much easier to decode especially as I have grown used to the pattern of her phrasing so it is possible for guesses to fill in any gaps. How could I possibly have failed to recognise him? Very frustrating for him. What must he think of me?

And yet the whole incident was entirely logical. I had no inkling they were about to contact me. Even more important, I wouldn't have expected them to be offering to send a map. So their call was a surprise and so was the reason for it. Without foreknowledge I had no basis on which to make guesses that would make any sense out of the lumps of audio porridge that caught me completely off-balance.

I have spent a lifetime using the phone and can no longer do so. Clearly I am missing something. But, instead of regretting the loss, I have tried to look at what I am able to do in its place. My first big discovery has been that I don't need to feel any pressure because I can't use it. (It would be very different if I was trying to hold down a job but life is different now that I am retired.) If the phone rings I no longer feel either the urge or the duty to answer it. It is not the end of the world. I can be comfortable with a different tempo. Phones are for other people. My normal life is without phones and people who matter to me and to whom I am important seem to understand that my normal is different from theirs. What I put in its place is a bit of a challenge but here again the beauty is that I am free to think of using my time and my life in a different way. Yes of course there are digital aids that can help me – email and text messages are perfect – but my biggest freedom comes from building a whole new way of thinking about the phone. I don't have to feel guilty about being unable to use it. Of course I don't want to miss important messages but if people want to get through to me and if I need to reach them then we will always find some way to connect.

However, I am well aware that my feeling about telephones would be very different if I was living entirely on my own. Phone calls are an almost essential channel for many routine activities to say nothing of emergencies. Could I afford to ignore them? Yes I probably could where time is not critical. E-mail, text messages and even the normal post are often sufficiently effective. And here again technology offers a number of other helpful alternatives. For example the text-phone system shows on a screen in front of me the words that a caller is saying while at the same time allowing me to respond in the normal way as soon as I understand what is being said. This would doubtless be among the suggestions that would be offered to me by one of the charity helplines or by a hearing therapist if I lived a more solitary lifestyle without the loving support that I receive from Tricia and other members of my family.

Tricia – *Telephones*

Comparatively recently telephones have become a big problem for John although luckily they did not become so until after he had retired. We have tried a huge selection to find one that works for him. When I was recently clearing out the loft Cancer Research became the surprised recipients of at least eight abandoned instruments. As recommended in RNID's magazine *One in Seven* he even got one with very big letters – although more appropriate for people who can't see normally, it has controls for volume and tone which, sadly, didn't help as well as he had hoped they would. Eventually he invested in a top of the range Bang & Olufsen model. It cost about the same as a goodish laptop and has hi-fi frequencies. With a new hearing aid he is able to use it with a few selected people mostly members of the family. He finds the sound quality in the earpieces of cheaper 'standard' phones too poor for him to decode. Those of us with normal hearing apparently compensate for the limited quality without thinking about it and there is clearly no big demand for anything better which lets manufacturers off the hook. He has also discovered that he hears quite well with his mobile – perhaps the two digital systems work well together.

His difficulty when using the telephone also points up the huge variations and problems of a lot of telephone manners. Call centres staffed by people

Hearing for John

with localised English accents in India, Ireland or Scotland can all be difficult even for those of us with good hearing. Add to this the far from straightforward computer-generated keying-in routines and you have the perfect recipe for a tantrum.

Another problem is that when John thinks of making a call he wants to make it now. That means he wants me to make it now even if I am in the middle of doing something else. We are learning to compromise on this. But perhaps the worst problems come up when he needs to talk to a secure place like a bank. I start the conversation by explaining that my husband will not be able to hear the person on the other end and that I will act as a go-between.

The standard requirement is that the answers to the security questions will have to come from John himself. We have a good routine going on this with a receiver each. 'What is your mother's maiden name?' the bank asks. I repeat the question, John gives the answer and we get through the open sesame that way.

However, there is one bank which has decided that I should not be able to hear John's answers and, worse, that I should not be trusted with the questions either. A really officious, though doubtless well-intentioned, woman conducted a conversation that went like this:

Hearing for John

Me: *'As my husband is deaf, I will repeat your questions and he will give you the answers.'*

Her: *'I'm afraid that is in contravention to our security procedures. You should not be in a position to hear either the questions I ask or the answers he gives. I suggest you move to a different room in order to be out of earshot.'*

(Protracted wrangling between her and me)

John: *'I am quite happy for my wife to hear both the questions and answers. She probably knows them all anyway.'*

Her: *'Oh no, that won't do at all. Mrs. Mills please get off the line.'*

Me: *'OK, I'm going out of the room now.'*

(I make stage footstep noises up and down the carpet)
Officious woman asks the first question.
I mouth it at John. He gets it wrong. I try again.

Her: *'Mrs. Mills, I think you are still on the line. You must get off the line.'*

Suppressing hysterical laughter I continue mouthing the questions. John guesses most of them, although not necessarily in the correct order.

Unfortunately the Officious Woman has a trick question which he cannot lipread. I try scribbling it down but he is in a bit of a panic, not to say a fury, and can't read my writing. Eventually he gets it right, I stage manage my footsteps back, and the conversation proceeds.

It has taken more than ten minutes to get to the point of John being able to ask a simple question about his account (phone call paid by us, of course).

John – *Life goes on, we go with it*

Do I lead a normal life socially? In many ways definitely yes, thanks largely to the tolerance and helpful understanding of friends. With people I know well I can feel comfortable about their willingness to make an effort to bridge the gaps. And even with new acquaintances the connection is usually easy to establish after the first few minutes during which they try to work out what problems my hearing loss is likely to cause them and I get used to the pitch of their voices and their ways of speaking – the 'music' of their conversation.

Their understanding and support can sometimes be extraordinary. On one occasion I was standing between two very new acquaintances, swivelling my head left and right to focus on their faces as they batted the conversation between them. Then came the inevitable moment when I missed something and I automatically apologised blaming my poor hearing. They were both friendly about it but, in addition, the chap on my right immediately moved to stand directly in front of me.

'That's really kind,' I told him gratefully. 'When did you learn to do that?' I half-expected him to mention a friend or member of his family with problems similar to mine.

He smiled. 'Not difficult,' he said. 'I am a doctor.'

I cannot think of any other doctor who I have met socially who has so carefully done anything similar to help me.

It's clear that those of us with hearing loss can feel reasonably confident that people will react positively

Hearing for John

when they know about our problems. Despite this there are social situations that I consciously dodge. After a game of tennis or golf I sometimes avoid the get-together for a drink and a chat. Why? Probably because I'm afraid that my hearing loss will kill the spontaneity and because I won't be able to enjoy the fun remarks that are so usual in this kind of unplanned socialising where the conversation is not only cheerful but noisy – too noisy for me to be able to keep up. That is the fear. Should I give in to it? Or should I brazen it out putting the onus on them to make sure that I feel included? I am still trying to work this out.

Hearing loss need not cut us off unless we allow it to. We need to see what it is doing to us so that we can build up a picture of the kind of person we have become because of it. One of the first steps is to make a list of things that we find challenging and face each one realistically, trying if possible to ignore the feelings of frustration that they cause in us.

So what are the main challenges? Here are some of the most obvious ones that affect me:
- Telephone
- Music
- TV and radio
- Theatre, concerts, opera
- Social chat – especially in noisy surroundings
- Meetings and speeches
- Official messages especially safety in aircraft, trains etc.
- Guided tours
- Exercise classes
- Learning with groups.

Hearing for John

What kind of feelings come out of these challenges?
- Stress
- Anger and resentment
- Frustration
- Irritation
- Jealousy
- Hopelessness
- Indifference
- Loss of self-respect
- Living second hand
- Being ignored
- Being patronised.

Many of us don't seem willing to talk about our problem. We hold it inside and do everything we can to hide the anxieties it causes us. Big mistake! Sharing it, talking it through openly and regularly allows other people to be part of it. Inevitably there are some who will be too impatient or bloody-minded to bother. But there are many others who will want to do anything they can to adapt their contact skills to minimise the effect which hearing problems cause us. Sympathetic relationships create the chance of finding solutions both for us and for other people. Some of my best hearing aids are people.

A new focus is the key, teaching ourselves to be open to new ideas, making sure that our mindset is constantly on the look out for interests and activities that will match more closely the changes in our abilities. In other words we need a completely fresh take on how we view everything. Once we do this it is amazing how quickly we notice the new choices and equally amazing how many there are. It's like switching off a light that illuminated one end of a room and switching on another one at the other end to discover a whole array of excitements that have been sitting there in the dark simply because we have not shone the beam of our focus on them. Art, reading, photography, writing, archaeology, surfing the internet, computer games, chess, card games, walking, jogging – do we need to go on? Even the most competitive sports can remain firmly in our orbit.

There is a huge amount we can do for ourselves especially if we are not too proud or too sensitive to enlist the support of family, friends, work colleagues and, even on occasions, total strangers.

Different hearing is a challenge that we are entitled to meet in any way that improves our connections with people whose hearing is regarded as 'normal'. We have to allow ourselves to be flexible in our thinking and in our emotions. Some doors close – that happens anyway because life never stays exactly the same from moment to moment. But for every door that shuts another one opens beckoning us towards totally new aims and possibilities.

The more we try to deliberately notice how well we are doing the more we give our confidence a big boost. Is the glass half-full or half-empty? Which one should we choose?

Tricia – *Shades of difference*

It's interesting to get a taste of what it's like to mishear and what it can do to the whole meaning of a conversation. Juan-Jesús speaks quite good English but with a very strong Spanish accent. The conversation turned to travel and I made some remark about how useless I had found a guide book to Spain designed for English users.

Juan-Jesús agreed enthusiastically. 'For example the new guide book for Madrid,' he said earnestly, 'it talks only about bacon.'

'You mean it ignores the Prado, the….' I tried to remember why Madrid should have any important connection with the pork industry.

'Yes, it is ridiculous. The museums, the beautiful buildings, they say nearly nothing. It is all bacon.'

Something in the way he pronounced 'bacon' the second time made me pause before sharing details of our agreeable Sunday morning ritual. And, yes, a sentence later I realised we weren't talking about breakfast at all but about football and the inordinate amount of coverage given to David Beckham and his family following his move to Real Madrid.

John seems to manage perfectly well on his own. He has drinks with his special mates, goes off to tennis regularly, and plays golf. This last is particularly challenging because some of his regular companions have broad Scottish accents but he seems to get on all right and is always included in their lunches.

Hearing for John

We're truly heartened and touched by the concern and tolerance of good friends one of whom is particularly determined to crack John's problem and is always bringing news cuttings and even little gadgets in the hope that they will help.

There are others who are not even aware that any support is needed. One day I was trying to identify John to a girl who formed part of his tennis group. 'He's deaf,' I said.

She looked at me uncomprehendingly. Just then he loomed into view and I pointed him out. 'Oh *him*,' she said. 'That's tall John. I've never thought of him as deaf.'

John – *Some do's and don'ts*

Fortunately we live in an age in which there is growing awareness and tolerance of hearing loss. Once again it is attitude that counts: theirs and mine. My attitude needs to emphasise the good bits of my life, the contributions I can make to the lives of others, the way my involvement can give them something extra. Everyone has problems. Self-concern is a never-ending topic. First person singular usually comes top of every personal agenda. Therefore any empathy I can show, any sympathy and help that I can offer, will have considerable impact if it is clear that I am also dealing with a big personal challenge.

How do I live the total package? First, by working out who I am and what place I feel I occupy in the awareness of others. Family, friends, work colleagues, casual strangers all have different reasons for interacting with me. I need to show understanding and gratitude for any help they try to give me and I must make certain that my own attitude to my difficulty is positive. It is important to work out a good balance between openness and the danger of making a self-serving thing of it. The simple act of sharing helps to build a bridge between us especially when the other bloke thinks he knows me but can't quite remember why.

'Did you buy the hybrid?' I ask him. Last time we met he really impressed me with his praise for the Toyota Prius. In his view green cars are what we all should be aiming for.

Hearing for John

He has been doing lengths in the swimming pool and I have just finished a work-out in the gym. The good thing about our club is the easy way we can chat even when we don't know each other very well. It never seems to matter if I have to go through the 'sorry can't hear you' routine. They're always very understanding. Hardly surprising. In the locker room there's usually someone putting on an elbow or knee guard or even juggling a pair of crutches. Sports injuries are common enough so with my hearing loss I am seldom the only one with a problem.

His mouth moves. But the rush of shower water and the echo of the tiled walls are totally blotting out the words. *'Wrieshorr mowie corris doy mmmmble,'* is all that comes through to me. Doesn't help that half the time he has a towel in front of his face.

I offer a smile that I hope is reassuring. *'Can't hear,'* I tell him with an apologetic shake of my head. *'Don't wear my hearing aid in here.'* I gesture at the shower heads. *'Electronics don't like water very much.'*

He looks seriously impressed and tries again. *'Ampishloononly woofle mmmbly.'*

I shake my head. *'No good.'* He looks abashed so I add apologetically: *'Probably shouldn't have started the conversation in here. I really just wanted to say hallo.'*

We had only met once before over a drink. I certainly wouldn't have expected him to remember that I am deaf. Even if he had it is unlikely he would have used a simple nod and thumbs up to give an answer. That kind of elementary sign language only becomes instinctive when you have practice dealing regularly with hearing problems. However all is not lost. He does make a small gesture which tells me that he appreciates that I have tried to connect.

Minutes later in the locker room I switch on my hearing aid. *'Contact,'* I tell him as he puts on his sock. *'Sorry about that. But did you get it?'* The sock stops mid-ankle. His face is a mask. I remind him. *'The Toyota?'* None of my business of course but I am really curious.

Immediately he relaxes and grins. *'Not yet. It's on order.'* He pulls the sock up the rest of the way. *'There's a bit of a queue.'* The tension's gone and the atmosphere between us is suddenly friendlier. His memory seems to have filled in the gap about our last meeting. More importantly he is obviously relieved I have at last heard and understood him. He doesn't mind that I am deaf. But he definitely felt uncomfortable about not getting through to me. Not that it was my fault. He just didn't have a clue what to do about it.

It's a lesson that I always try to remember. Building these vital bridges depends on how understanding and helpful I can be. I'm the one who has all the practice. I'm the one who knows about my hearing loss and I should never assume anyone has noticed or has any idea how to handle it. Therefore it is all up to me; it can be very rewarding to use my experience to make the connection work.

So how do I compensate for the way hearing loss sometimes makes me seem distant, even aloof and unapproachable? How do I build the bridge that will save others having to make an extra effort every time they are with me? Equally important how can I avoid the 'idiot eagerness' that some people with hearing loss use to signal that they are keen to grab any opportunity to establish contact?

While making sure that I am not trying to hide anything the first step is to relax and act 'normally'. Easier to say than to do. If it works well they may be surprised to discover that I have any problem at all – this is quite common. But as soon as there is any difficulty I explain without any hesitation or feeling of embarrassment. How I hear is different from them and it is in their interests as well as mine to establish common ground.

For all that let's be specific. How do I handle people who either don't understand or deliberately don't attempt to recognise my hearing loss because they are too busy, too impatient, too uncaring, too mean-spirited, too self-absorbed and totally disinterested?

1. I face the problem squarely. I do not ask or hope for patience or sympathy. I accept that my relationship with them has a problem and if it is going to be put right I will have to do all the work because they can't or don't want to.
2. I pay attention to the way they are behaving and try to understand the reasons for their attitude. If I can work it out then I have a better chance of making constructive moves that will build a bridge between us.
3. I decide how important they are to me. Does it suit me and is it in my interests to continue the contact and use my experience to make it work? If not I can politely break the connection and move on.
4. I explain to them clearly the ways in which, from my point of view, my hearing loss is affecting the

Hearing for John

contact. Equally important I tell them how much I am aware of the problems that this is causing for them so that they can see I am sympathetic to any frustrations, irritations and unwelcome weight they are feeling. And, yes, I can apologise. Why not? Of course it's not my fault. But, if the contact is important enough, no point in allowing false pride to get in the way.

5. I suggest some ideas for them to try to get through to me:
    - They can speak slower and more deliberately but *not* necessarily louder – I should explain that louder sometimes makes it more difficult to understand the words.
    - They can try to make sure that whenever they are speaking I can see their face and most importantly their mouth so that I can lipread. In this context, they may not realise that it is going to be difficult for me if they stand with their back to the light so that their face is in shadow or if they wave their hands in front of their face.
    - When there are difficult phrases or ideas maybe they should spell them or write them down so that I can understand what the conversation is all about. Too often it is difficult to follow ideas not only because I can't decode the words but because I don't really know what everyone's talking about.
    - When I am in tune with a subject even though I may not hear all the words I can nevertheless use guesses to fill in the gaps and keep up with

Hearing for John

the gist of things. In an ideal world I might suggest moving to a quieter environment so that they do not have to compete with the noises in the background.
- I might also tell them that the background music is making it hard to understand what they are saying. Constant music is so much a part of life for many people they often don't even notice it is playing. And yet it is taking up valuable space in my hearing aid making it difficult for the sounds of voices to get through.

On the other side of the coin how do I show people who do care that their efforts are appreciated? How do I repay them for taking the trouble?

1. I tell them and show them by the warmth of my reactions and make a point of saying thank you – not once but quite regularly. However I take special care to avoid being too eager and too pathetically grateful.
2. I focus carefully on what they are doing and saying so that I have the best possible chance of keeping up with them and don't have to constantly ask for words and ideas to be repeated or explained.
3. I tell them without hesitation what is working for me and what is not so that they have a chance to fine tune their efforts
4. I show how much the contact means to me by adding constructively in any way I can to the ideas that I am involved in with them. I do my best to show interest in things that interest them – which of course is just good manners.

5. I recognise that it can be hard for them and so when, as often happens, they don't get through I don't labour the subject. Instead I let it go for now and try to find a gap to catch up with it later.
6. I *do not* allow my disappointment, fatigue or frustration to show when the contact is not working for me. I don't withdraw into an uncomprehending corner. Instead I try to behave normally and pleasantly as though I am still fully engaged until the contact starts to work for me again.

However in my attempts to stay in the loop there are times when the way I use my voice becomes, to say the least, abnormal. When I can't hear myself clearly I wind up the volume of my voice until I can. Against the competition of loud background noise in supermarkets, restaurants, trains or even keeping up an animated conversation while walking energetically I somehow can't avoid the embarrassing habit of talking too loudly. No matter how hard I try I find it is nearly impossible to get the balance right. When it happens I reduce the power of my sound waves to a level that I judge is more discreet. The only problem is I can never know if I have got it right and even the reassurance of companions does little to reduce my uncertainty.

Hearing our own voice is a vital part of the way we live. The sound is familiar and we learn quite early in life how to manage it to reflect emotions and inject special emphasis. If we ever have difficulty hearing it clearly it not only becomes harder to be sure about projecting the nuances that we intend. It can also feel physically disorientating. It can seriously affect the confidence we

Hearing for John

feel in our conversations and it may even change the way we use our voice.

This sometimes happens with people who lose all hearing. The way they form their words and the character of the sound that they project becomes noticeably different. Does it matter? Not at all so long as the message they are trying to convey is understood. That is always going to be the bottom line test.

Tricia – *Feedback*

'Am I speaking too loudly?' John has learned to ask this question regularly because there are times when he finds it difficult to know whether he is shouting or mumbling especially in a noisy restaurant or with friends in an animated conversation. As he becomes more emphatic about some favourite topic or argument the volume of his projection tends to rise, sometimes well above the surrounding sounds of background babble or even heavy road traffic. People at neighbouring tables, and some even as much as half a restaurant away, have been known to take a close interest which can be embarrassing when the subject is juicy gossip or something very personal.

At first to help him understand that he should reduce volume I used to make small downward movements with my hands which distracted him greatly. It also usually made him lose the thread of his argument which irritated him even more. Now he has become better at gauging how loudly he is speaking and is more aware of any sudden attention from an uninvited audience. Playing safe he sometimes speaks so quietly that even those of us with the best of hearing struggle to make sense of what he is saying.

He is usually quite cheerful about it because he understands that it is not entirely his fault. He has worked out that, as a result of the millions of calculations it processes every second to deal with the constantly changing cocktail of incoming sounds, the hard-working hearing aid makes decisions that may

Hearing for John

well be digitally ideal for the environment but can be quite unsuitable for the kind of hearing that he needs. If that's a downside he's happy to live with it and enjoy the other benefits which are many.

John – *How to stay connected*

The more practised I become in handling my hearing problems the more I notice the reactions they seem to cause. Raised eyebrows, an amused grin, a frown of confusion, a scowl of frustration: should I take them to heart or are they really only caused by the difficulty of getting through to me? The difference is crucial. Unless I think carefully about this every time it happens I may come to the wrong conclusion which will put a strain on the relationship. I must do everything I can to be sure I have the right answer. With family and close friends, where there is daily contact, it should be relatively easy to decide. With other people it may be more difficult but the more alert I am in trying to spot the difference the better chance I will have of getting the right message.

How do I handle it? Simple. I always assume that they are doing their best to get through and that any negatives in their face or body language are caused by their own anxiety about failing to connect with me. This makes me feel warm about them and so I act positively. My attitude usually helps them to feel better. Of course I don't always make the right assumption but, if they are being angry or moody, it quickly shows in other ways.

And then how do I handle those times when I seem to be excluded from what is going on simply because I can't hear? Is there any way of being better involved, especially in conversations?

Hearing for John

So often when I'm in a group I notice that one or more of them is looking in my direction to see whether I am hearing what is going on. They have no way of knowing how much or how little is getting through to me. It would be so much easier for them if they could be confident that I will let them know whenever the connection isn't working. I need to remember it is my responsibility not only to myself but also to them to make sure I stay connected.

The first and probably most proactive step in this direction is establishing that everyone involved knows I have a hearing problem and how severe it is. They won't necessarily have noticed that I am wearing a hearing aid – surprising how often they don't – and I can't assume they have remembered my hearing loss if we have met before. There is no need for any embarrassment. I want their help and the best way to get it is to be absolutely open up front. Whatever I say needs to be simple and friendly.

Then I tell them how I plan to alert them whenever my connection with them fails. This is the key question both for me and for them especially in a formal meeting where I am expected to be an active contributor. They will almost certainly react positively if I explain that I would like to use a simple routine. Some kind of gesture or hand movement is one possibility but it's hard to be sure that they will see it every time. Far better to have one or two words that act like a code. For example: *'Excuse me'*, or *'replay please'*, or *'no contact'*, or *'didn't hear that'*.

This is exactly the opposite of the way in which a hard-pressed executive of my acquaintance is handling

Hearing for John

his progressively pronounced hearing loss. In social conversations he misses quite a lot. But far worse is his worry that in business meetings, which are a very big part of his crowded schedule, he finds that he frequently doesn't pick up vital points and has to rely on some of his colleagues to fill in the gaps. Equally important is the effect on his levels of stress. The anxiety of not being sure how much he is missing combines with an irritation (sometimes even anger) about people who seem to be mumbling or deliberately speaking too quietly – emotionally a lethal cocktail that can have a big impact on his enthusiasm and the way he performs. He is in denial, unwilling to make a fuss. And yet in time he will have to have a hearing aid. But with it or without it his interaction with business colleagues would be a great deal easier for him and for them if he could keep his problem clearly on the table like one of the regular items on their meeting agendas.

Once a simple routine has been accepted the interruptions it causes should be minimal even become 'part of the furniture'. Obviously there is a difference in the way we handle a formal meeting compared with a social group. But in both our success depends on how well we make everyone aware of our need for help. If we can be very confident and open we immediately cut down the risk of other people feeling that they have to tread carefully to avoid hurting our feelings. We want them to know about and accept our problem so they can handle it in their own way without any fear of embarrassment on either side. This is a great way of building bridges.

Tricia – *Lost in transmission*

Over the years I have learned to appreciate more and more how much John has to rely on facial expressions and body language to understand people. I have also discovered to my cost how often my face, without any malicious intent on my part, frequently sends totally the wrong message to him. For example there are times when he accuses me of looking furious. He is convinced that I am extremely angry when in reality I am only trying to get my message across. This can be upsetting to say the least.

I've tried replicating my expressions in front of the mirror and have come to the conclusion that for John this is yet another foreign language:

Leaving me	**Reaching John**
caring and concerned	angry
emphatic	belligerent
thoughtful	sulky
enthusiastic	taken leave of my senses
desperation	I hate you, divorce imminent
I *need* to get through	frustrated scowl

Perhaps I need a short course on facial linguistics.

John – *Never the same twice?*

At night I stow the aid in a specially-designed dehumidifier which helps to make sure that moisture does not find its way into the system and affect the overall performance. Next morning I switch on again and very often the sound I am expecting, based on what I got used to during the previous day and evening, is not quite the sound the instrument now seems to deliver. Some confusion ensues especially during the first cup of morning coffee when conversation is difficult enough anyway. Audiologists tell me it is likely that any small changes are caused by my ear or my overall mood. If I wake up bright and breezy my hearing will be clear and sharp. After a less than restful night I will start fatigued with a slower pace, and my reduced alertness will affect the way I am hearing.

And yet I don't remember this kind of experience with my earlier analogue aids. Their performance was more consistent. Perhaps the sound quality was not as sharp; fine tuning may not have been as flexible and precise. But my ear and my brain could rely on handling the same volume and quality of input every time. The predictable continuity was very reassuring and allowed my brain enough time to develop its own ways of reacting. I experienced many years of near normality without constantly worrying about how the aid was going to perform for the next change of scene.

Dare I risk a heresy? Is a digital hearing aid a total blessing or does it cause its own special difficulties? Clearer, sharper, every frequency perfectly defined, yet

Hearing for John

it is not as gentle and forgiving as the ear itself. How and what I hear depends on how the instrument is set up, how well my needs have been understood and translated into the options that the aid is offering me. Perfect it can never be. Approximate, close perhaps but inevitably there will be unexpected even unusable results.

Are the digital systems too complicated? Have the makers devised sufficiently simple foolproof routines to help hearing professionals find the best possible individual settings accurately and quickly? My personal experience has been that the almost limitless permutations leave considerable room not only for experiments but also, much more worryingly, for errors. Hearing aid audiologists seem to need a special combination of technical know-how and dogged detective work to achieve their best results – which sometimes come from inspired guesswork. As with everything else connected with hearing there is no absolutely precise way of measuring and solving problems.

If the aid has been incorrectly set up (no matter how small the error) my life – yes, my whole life – is affected. I am the only one who knows what flavour of sound really suits me. And yet I am powerless to fine-tune the programme settings. That option is not offered with digital hearing aids. I have to seek help from a professional and there are not enough of them to meet demand. In any case time and other commercial constraints make it difficult for them to give me unlimited personal attention.

Hearing for John

With all the sophisticated technology built into digital hearing aids why has it not been possible to devise some system that will allow me to do at least some of my own simple fine-tuning? Hi-fi systems and even ordinary television sets offer this flexibility. Digital cameras give us the freedom to adjust the number of recorded pixels, colour saturation, contrast, white balance and many of the other basics. Surely it is not too much to ask for us to be trusted with something similar in a hearing aid? I readily admit that there will be many users who may not wish to take advantage of this kind of facility either because they feel it will be too complicated or too much of a nuisance. (They may also prefer simple point and click with their camera.) But there are many others, like me, with long track records for whom this extra dimension could be beneficial. And if it worked as well as it should think how much valuable professional time we could save.

When I explained this problem to the distributor of one of the most progressive and innovative hearing aid systems I received a very interesting response which is well worth quoting here:

A key fact to consider is the nature of hearing and the way the brain adapts and re-adapts to new stimuli. You will certainly know that people adapt relatively quickly to a new spectacle prescription. But it takes the brain longer to adapt to a new amplification prescription, even though it may be appropriate for the newly measured hearing loss and the overall need for speech intelligibility. Therefore we often need to get the wearer to become accustomed to the optimum amplification over a period of time before we consider making further adjustments at the next scheduled appointment. This gives the brain time to habituate to the new sounds.

Thus hearing aid manufacturers are trying to maintain a compromise position between what the majority of users want, which is a discreet, highly automated device that requires minimal user intervention, and the needs of a more experienced minority, who desire maximum flexibility and would like to be more in control of the many parameters. But in a commercial world, we all have to walk the line between ease of use for the many and complexity for the few, while keeping everything neat, small and not power-hungry. It's quite a tall order.

The distributor also added that new devices are already being developed capable of gradually self-learning a user's preferred volume setting. Also in the future there may well be designs that meet our desire for greater personal control more fully. I feel we have good reason to be optimistic.

Tricia – *Games of care*

Living with a deaf person can be a bit like living by yourself. By that I mean I have to hear for both of us just as if I were the sole incumbent of the estate. If I hear a strange noise which indicates that something unpleasant is happening in or around the house there is no point in ignoring it in the hope that John will hear it and do something about it – he won't, because he can't. Same thing applies to the doorbell, the telephone, the person wandering up the drive looking for a non-existent house number – it's me or nobody. Doubly difficult if it's something I don't know how to deal with – like a constant trickly water noise in the toilet while John is in the middle of something intellectually important on the computer and any interruption to his train of thought may be calamitous. Which do I risk: consigning to oblivion for ever that stroke of genius trembling on the threshold of his mind or the collapse of the ceiling as the trickle upstairs suddenly becomes an uncontrollable flood?

This does mean of course that I can act as if I do live alone without getting strange looks. I can mutter or sing to myself, burp noisily or sniff uncontrollably. John is none the wiser. The trouble with this is that it can be a bit antisocial when other people are around. Samantha's friend Louisa calls my unconscious wall-to-wall rendering of Carmen's Toreador 'inverted whistling' and I now realise that this happy sound plays quite a large part in my daily round. I also need to remember to stop telling myself out loud what I am going to do next.

Another by-product of living with someone deaf is that you develop special codes and mannerisms. People are surprised at the contortions I go to in order to stay on their left side while walking with them – quite unnecessary of course when they have two good ears. And tennis has become a whole new ball game (sorry). A 'let' is signalled by a two-finger salute; instead of calling a ball 'out' or 'long' I do an imitation of an overweight swan trying to get airborne and so on. Again this tends to spill over into games with 'normal' hearing people who cannot understand why I have become bereft of speech and am cavorting about the court in such an unseemly manner.

Occasionally, just very occasionally, I think, 'Lucky John, not having to hear this'. We were at a post-wedding party, a disco. The music was excruciatingly loud. He was boogying away with a happy expression on his face. 'Don't try talking to me,' he mouthed. 'I'm switched off.'

Asleep in bed without his hearing aid John is 'dead to the world'. Sometimes the consequences have been quite comic. About 2am one morning I was woken up by what I thought was the alarm clock but which turned out to be the front door bell. From one of the windows I could see our next-door neighbour plus two uniformed policemen trying to unlock our front door.

They explained that the burglar alarm central station had phoned to say that our telephone line had gone dead indicating possible foul play by intruders. What had actually happened was that a new phone,

Hearing for John

bought to help John's hearing, had somehow messed up the system. We unplugged the offending phone which restored normal service and I went back to bed.

In the morning John asked me how I had slept. 'How about you?' I asked before replying. 'I had a really good night,' he said happily.

John – *Accepting reality*

Some things are quite clear to me now although for anyone who is not directly involved with hearing loss they may not be obvious.

First, and most important, treating deafness is not an exact science. There are no easy answers and seemingly none of them is precise. None of us experiences sounds in identically the same way as anyone else. Hearing is particular and very personal and I have learned how difficult it is for even the best professional expertise and technology to supply ideal solutions.

On one occasion I was part of an obedient small party of sightseers following a raised umbrella mingling with all the other raised umbrellas. We left behind the hot sun and traffic noise and entered the cool gloom of a lofty cathedral. Gathering around our guide we waited for her to continue her commentary. So far throughout the morning I had managed to be close to the front row in order to hear her and others in our party had kindly made space for me. Despite all the usual competition from the din of the busy streets I had managed quite well. My digital programme, set to reduce background noise, had been working far better than I had dared to hope for. Now with all those noises shut outside the great heavy cathedral doors I assumed I wouldn't need to be quite so close to her. But I couldn't have been more wrong!

I watched her face as she started. Her lips moved. But I heard her only as though from a very great distance. The words were difficult most of them actually impossible

Hearing for John

to decode. I checked my hearing aid. The programme setting was the same. I increased the volume. It made little difference. Her voice level scarcely changed. Was I going mad? In the street I could hear her in spite of the noise. Here, in the reverential quiet, she was now, to me, almost inaudible. And no, she was not using a hushed sepulchral tone. Her performance seemed identical to the one she was delivering outside. What on earth was going on?

I pondered for the rest of the day and finally arrived at the answer. I had assumed that in the quiet of the church there would be no problem. That was my big mistake. The size of the interior made it appear to be quiet. But it was not. The huge vaulted spaces were filled with a host of noises that chorused together in an enormous jumbled echo. There is only a limited amount of space for sound in my hearing aid and that echo had taken up most of it. No wonder it was hard to hear her.

Easier to understand was my experience of sitting with friends at an outside table on a warm summer evening. As usual the voices of other diners together with the usual restaurant background made it hard for me to follow the conversation. I managed tolerably well except that, from time to time, the hearing aid seemed to cut out totally for a few seconds before resuming normal service. It was only as the evening progressed that the reason emerged. As my hearing blacked out for the tenth time one of my friends looked up in frustration at the dark sky and remarked that flights to Heathrow were coming in very low. Flights? I hadn't realised there

Hearing for John

were any. The sound from the jet engines was so loud that my hearing aid had freaked out.

For anyone wearing a hearing aid sound experiences can be a huge drain on physical and emotional energy. Many things don't sound like they used to, seldom better, often worse. Wooden chair legs screech mercilessly on a tiled floor. Kitchen pans, especially roasting pans, have a brand of clatter that would earn them a place in the torturers' hall of fame. A builder using a power tool to cut a paving stone triggers in my mind the shrill of an ambulance klaxon. Floor to ceiling windows, shiny walls and floors deliver chattering echoes that the aid does nothing to dampen – it often does exactly the opposite. Unfair to condemn the marvels of the digital system except that it can so easily exaggerate the extremes and my ear's usually forgiving cushion cannot cope. How can anyone with normal hearing possibly understand how infuriating and exhausting this can be? Too much sound is always worse than too little. In self-defence I sometimes switch off totally for a few moments and breathe deeply in the hope that when I activate the system again it will have found a fresh way to interpret the inputs. It seldom does.

Some publicity suggests that the digital system can soften the extremes because it thinks for itself. Quite possibly and miraculously it does but what good is this if it doesn't think the way I need it to? The basic idea is that the digital brain should change raw sounds into a form that my brain will find is helpful. Yet this does not avoid the problem that two brains, the aid's and mine, will be reacting separately to the same inputs. There are inevitably going to be times when they work

Hearing for John

against each other and whenever this happens my hearing experience will be difficult.

It's all very personal. And, as always in dealing with hearing loss, so much depends on the skills of the professionals. So it is perhaps worth reminding ourselves who they are:

- *Ear, nose and throat specialists*
- *Hearing aid designers and manufacturers*
- *Hearing aid audiologists and dispensers*
- *Hearing therapists*
- *Lipspeakers*
- *BSL/English teachers*

At the end of this book there is a list of some helpful sources of information.

The chances of finding a perfect match between us and them so that we understand each other exactly and can work towards achieving the best possible results are not very high. The best we can hope for is something quite close. This is the reality. Understanding this, and accepting the limitations it creates, is essential if both the customer/patient and the professional are to get the best out of their efforts to solve problems.

Sadly too many of us who are customers start our relationship with expectations that are too high which lead to disappointments, frustrations and a certain amount of disillusionment. Whereas we may have been hoping for a 100% rapport, we quickly learn that if we get anywhere above 50% we are lucky and doing well. Once we accept this and genuinely understand what it means we can adjust our expectations.

Are the professionals on our side – always? On the face of it of course. But they expect us to accept

Hearing for John

compromises and not to aim for the impossible. *'We can't make you hear perfectly. We can only make you hear better.'* How much the 'better' satisfies our hopes is always going to be a very personal question.

Tricia – *Tale of the unexpected*

Sunday morning. I am luxuriating in the bath thinking of nothing in particular when I become aware of a jangling noise. Next door's burglar alarm? The restaurant across the road? Or *our* burglar alarm? I leap out of the bath, grab a towel and run dripping into the bedroom where I find John, minus his hearing aid, happily humming a little tune.

He looks surprised to see me. 'The alarm's gone off!' I yell at him lunging for the phone to tell Banham's it's a false alarm. No good. While making our bed John has inadvertently hit the panic button which means the police come anyway.

We throw on clothes and, sure enough, a couple of minutes later the local uniformed police force in the shape of our 'home beat' next door neighbour Mike and his mate come briskly into the drive looking suitably official and serious. We explain our silliness and Mike says kindly it was time for him to come home for breakfast anyway.

John – *Staying positive*

Then one day was more of a struggle. A familiar German voice on the phone had a hard time making me understand. I had come to think of Helmut as a friend, and yet somehow I just couldn't connect. Later our routine production meeting was ragged because of the number of points I missed or misheard. As a result my temper was not at its best which caused an equal reaction in other people at the table. I was thinking a lot about how well or badly I could hear and the more I thought about it the worse it seemed to get.

I thought back about the progression of my hearing loss.

In phase one I started by resisting any thoughts of deafness. I was largely unaware of what I was missing and in any case I put any lack of connection down to inattention and other pressures. I certainly did not recognise that my struggles to hear better were causing stress and fatigue which contributed to the irritability that for quite a long time became my professional trademark. It was a vicious circle as the stress itself affected the way I could hear.

Phase two started with a positive diagnosis of my hearing loss that forced me to look hard at the options. There was immediate anxiety about the future and quite a lot of damage to my self-confidence. My moods became sensitive to frustration with the inadequacy of my connections both professionally and socially. I began to have serious concerns about how I was going to cope which led me to accept, reluctantly, that I needed to follow the advice of the hearing professionals.

Hearing aids were the big step forward in phase three. To begin with it seemed that it would be impossible for me to come to terms with the new artificial sounds that they were delivering. More than ever now I was in the hands of the professionals, totally dependent upon their advice and yet strangely unwilling to trust them totally. How could I? I was not in control and hated the feeling. Worse still were sensations of self-blame and vulnerability. And then, in addition, there was the totally unexpected shock of the acoustic neuroma and the loss of all hearing in my right ear. With the left side already deteriorating, I was suddenly down to well below 50% of normality. But still I felt I was actually lucky. I could have had no hearing at all.

Phase four was a break-through. The hearing professionals proved to be right. With their encouragement my brain and I adapted very well to the new regime with analogue hearing aids and remarkably quickly too. Adjustments became a familiar part of my meetings with the dispenser. My comments and descriptions must have improved because they led him to make things better for me. At work and in all social settings I felt at ease. During fifteen very busy years I ran a small independent production company and directed high profile actors in recording character voices (with all their complicated nuances) for more than 150 episodes of children's animation for BBC TV and other broadcasters. I was able to use the phone and in every way follow my career normally. If my moods were sometimes scratchy my colleagues blamed pressure of work. They were only partly right. The demands of fighting to hear well with only one ear assisted by a hearing aid contributed in no small way to my stress.

Nevertheless I was almost proud to draw attention to my hearing loss especially when others clearly didn't notice and treated me as totally normal. I didn't even think of the word disability. How could I? All my achievements, thanks to the skills of the hearing professionals who were helping me, were positive and even progressive as my brain learned daily how to devise new ways to compensate.

That was then.

Now I was looking in the mirror and facing the latest challenge. It felt like the start of phase five and I had no idea where it was leading. What gave me this feeling? Instinct? Or was it a definite understanding that the hill was getting steeper? Decoding was noticeably harder. I was not doing nearly as well as I had been. Running out of energy or patience?

If I needed an excuse, I could easily find it in the latest audiogram. The curve of the graph now looked as though it had fallen off a cliff. I no longer reacted at all to any of the beeps in the upper frequencies (even though I guessed that I could detect a couple of faint ones) which might explain why, when we did the word recognition test, I scored zero.

Downhill definitely. But strangely enough it doesn't feel all that bad. Right now I still seem to be able to do all the things I have always done. I suppose the real differences I notice are in the extra efforts that people around me are making to help me keep up.

Tricia – *How to get out?*

I must never be without a key – simply because if I lock myself out of the house I will never get back in again by ringing the doorbell, hammering on the front door or phoning home on my mobile as John will not hear any of these. And, as he is frequently totally engrossed in what he is doing, it may be several hours, such as until lunchtime or drink time, before he notices I am missing.

Of course this could apply just as well if I was *inside* the house and had an accident which is why I usually try to be extra careful to avoid potential hazards that could leave me lying unconscious. But you can't cover everything. For instance one day I was just about ready to go for an interview at a primary school and nipped into the bathroom before leaving. When I tried to reopen the door the handle came off in my hand trapping me inside.

I knew John was downstairs somewhere well within earshot for anybody with normal hearing. But I also knew that a gentle little call for his attention would not do. I banged, I yelled, I thumped, I shrieked. I even tried to make enough noise to attract the next door neighbour should he be available. My deadline grew nearer. I do not like being late for interviews. My voice grew hoarse, the door threatened to cave in. Eventually I heard welcome footsteps coming slowly up the stairs. 'Did you call?' he asked innocently.

John – *Hiss and friends*

Most of us know how it feels to face an uninvited guest especially when the extra presence brings nothing but aggravation. Our only consolation may be that when the party is over the problem will go away. But what if we find that we have an intruder with whom we are going to have to spend the rest of our lives? Worse still we are going to share every waking and sleeping moment with this menace.

I can't remember exactly when I became aware that Hiss and friends had come to stay. Did they, in a cunning, underhand way, arrive in my life through the back door? Or did I let them in by allowing deafening blasts of sound to blow down the safety screens guarding my ears? I do clearly recall that as a raw young recruit on the Territorial Army rifle range I was ordered to fire seemingly endless rounds of .303 ammunition in target practice and that after each session the ringing in my ears persisted for some hours which later became several days. The use of a shotgun against pigeons and snakes in the African bush had the same effect. Ear plugs, never mind ear defenders, would have been seen as a sign of weakness had I even thought to ask for them, which I didn't. Was this the open sesame for my unwelcome guests or just the first hammer blows that would lead to my later loss of hearing?

If you are an old hand you will have instantly recognised that I am describing tinnitus. And if you have it you may also be familiar with the efforts that are constantly being made to find ways of helping you to

Hearing for John

manage it. The various sounds you are hearing are not generated by any outside agency: this is all that has been discovered so far. To prove this a number of experiments have shown that when people with normal hearing have been placed in a totally soundproof environment in which no sound waves could be detected they have reported 'hearing' noises. The conclusion has been that the 'sounds' can only have originated 'inside their heads'. Some researchers even suggest that we all have tinnitus but some of us have it more noticeably than others.

RNID has done a great deal to describe the causes, the research work that is being done and possible ways of relieving tinnitus. Very reassuringly they tell us that it is not a disease and not life-threatening even though, for some of us, it can be unpleasantly intrusive and frustratingly difficult to treat effectively.

In my personal experience Hiss and the gang are like members of a fancy dress party. They keep changing their costumes. Of course Hiss is always there as the anchor. I really don't notice him unless I think to 'listen'. But am I listening or is the presence just a trick of my auditory system mischievously playing games in partnership with some obscure and as yet undiscovered corner of my brain? For me Hiss is relatively friendly and not intrusive – doesn't keep me awake at night or make me feel depressed or irritated. But there are other sounds that are quite different. (Come to think of it can we call them sounds? As they are not generated by external vibrations and sound waves how can we?)

There are tweets and whistles. Some remind me of the interference that used to be quite common in the background of telephone calls – no longer there thanks

Hearing for John

to digital technology. Others include pulsing, even throbbing and they seem to be linked with moments of anxiety and stress. I have never known them to do me any harm and I have learned that if I deliberately ignore them they soon retire into the background even if they don't go away. Of course this is harder in the wee small hours when wakefulness causes all kinds of random thoughts to jostle for space. But even then I have sometimes found that by thinking beautiful thoughts unwanted noises in my head can be less annoying.

Is tinnitus caused by a badly functioning auditory nerve? Again the researchers have no firm conclusions. However I wonder if it can be. During the surgery to remove my acoustic neuroma the auditory nerve was unavoidably damaged which resulted in total loss of hearing in my right ear. And yet it is from that region of my head that I detect most of the noises that I associate with tinnitus even though the auditory nerve no longer has any function.

So, what's the answer? As far as I can see there isn't one yet. Certainly there is no easy solution that will allow me to get rid of my uninvited guests. However it is comforting to know that I am not alone with this problem and that a great deal of work is ongoing to find answers. Meanwhile I can only repeat that I find the best source of information is RNID and other leading charities. They offer a great deal of helpful, and in many ways comforting, background advice.

Tricia – *Progress of a sort?*

I recently heard a wonderful story about a hearing dog who had been trained to jump on its owner's bed if the smoke alarm went off. One night the dog did just this and the owner got out of bed and checked the alarm. No flashing lights, no smoke. She got back into bed, turned out the light. Minutes later a repeat performance. Still she found nothing. She reprimanded the dog and was just about to go back to sleep when she saw a glow outside and realised the house next door was on fire! It seems that this story is typical of the many new ways that are being worked out to get over hearing problems. How many of them will be needed in due course by John is anyone's guess.

I can't say that I have really noticed on a day-to-day basis that his hearing is getting worse. It is only when I look back that I am aware of how much life has changed and the impact this has had on me.

It is true that the bulk of the organisation of our activities now falls to me, 'the management' (as he labels me). This can work to my advantage although I really do try not to slant things my way – well hardly ever! But is this so different from the vast majority of couples? If I want to ring friends to set up a social date who controls the diary? And when planning a holiday is it so unusual for me to be the one who makes the detailed arrangements while he depletes his bank account and clears his desk?

Yes, I have sole responsibility for reacting to anything where sound is concerned including announcements at airports and train or underground stations as well as things that go bump in the night. But if John is out on his own there are perfectly good information boards as an alternative.

Yes, I'm the only one able to communicate by telephone including incoming calls but we can still contact each other providing we both have our mobiles and use the texting facility. And we don't for a moment forget the internet which has become John's lifeline for keeping in touch with family and friends and business contacts all over the planet, to say nothing of being a priceless source of information.

No, we can't really go to the cinema, the theatre, or a concert as a couple any more, but this gives me opportunities for an evening out with our daughter Samantha or a girlfriend.

So, of course we have challenges. But they're very far from insuperable.

John – *Looking forward*

Much of what I have described has been based on my experiences of hearing treatment in the private sector. However I believe that many of the views I have shared with you apply irrespective of the level hearing loss or treatment. We should perhaps look forward to wonder how soon (if ever) this kind of 'bespoke' service on demand can become a more easily affordable norm.

More hearing professionals? Lower-priced technology? Wider awareness of hearing problems leading, inevitably, to a more lively debate about what can be done? New action? Yes, all of these. And any improvements in the services offered by NHS, especially more frequent and regular access to essential after care, would make a big difference. So what should be the priorities?

Awareness comes first. For too long hearing loss has been relegated to a sympathy ghetto. Deafness has been an embarrassment in a way unique among all disabilities. This is changing and a new generation of innovative professionals can see exceptional opportunities in a potential mass market of 500 million customers worldwide. It is entirely possible that an explosion of budget level high street hearing aid dispensers may happen in a way similar to the changes that have given many of UK's opticians a very different high street profile. Can hearing care in shops ever be equal to the bespoke support that I have described in so many of these pages? No reason why not providing, in the case of the UK, the shortage of qualified hearing professionals can be remedied. At present they may be too thin on the ground to meet the demands of a mass market.

For the nine million of us who might have needed their services in 2006 there were no more than 2,800 audiologists working in the NHS. At the same time there were just over 1,500 private sector hearing aid dispensers and their employers throughout the UK. The number of students who qualified as dispensers during 2005 was only 112 – numbers trying to qualify actually dropped by more than 10% compared with the previous year.

Compare these figures with eye-care services (and remember that for most of us after-care for spectacles is usually far less time consuming than for hearing aids). In 2005/6 there were more than 10,400 registered optometrists and 5,200 registered dispensing opticians. In both disciplines the numbers entering the professions were showing a steady increase.

We shouldn't be surprised. If you are an optometrist or an optician everyone who wears spectacles is a walking advertisement for your work. Those frames and tinted lenses are image-building – especially the latest 'shades'. By contrast, even though hearing care services are beginning to be more widely advertised, hearing aids are designed to be hidden and hearing professionals, like doctors, have tended to keep their activities discreet. Why? Is hearing care more 'medical' than eye care?

Perhaps hearing aids will never become design accessories but surely those of us who wear them can afford to be more open, even proud of the way they improve the quality of our lives? Isn't it possible that a

Hearing for John

more positive posture in us will give more confidence and status to the hearing profession itself with benefits all round?

Should caring for hearing be more widely promoted as a rewarding, worthwhile career? From the point of view of a grateful customer/patient I would sincerely hope so. As an important first step the skills and qualifications certainly need to be better understood and recognised. For example, when a young audiologist asked for a quotation to insure his new car the insurance broker wanted to know about his profession. 'Audiologist' drew a blank. It was nowhere to be found on the insurance company register of job titles and had to be explained. Similarly on the NHS website in 2006 the page headed 'Welcome to NHS careers' listed Ambulance, Dental, Doctors, Health Informatics, Management, Nursing and others. No mention of audiology. To be fair, eyes weren't included either but the omission of audiology is all the more surprising because, for so many people with hearing problems, the NHS is their first and *only* port of call.

What needs to be done? Here again, awareness. Anyone looking for a new career will assess pay, job satisfaction and future prospects. It seems to me that the negative shadow that has hung over deafness for so many years may have clouded the idea of working with deaf and hard of hearing people. You need to be a certain kind of individual driven by 'higher motives' to want to help anyone who is disabled, don't you? Some kind of do-gooder? This is not true.

The reality is that with advanced technology and new attitudes the challenges of helping deaf and hard

Hearing for John

of hearing people to live normally can be extremely rewarding. Job satisfaction can be high. Prospects in this expanding market look good. New inventions and new treatments will offer opportunities to learn new skills and acquire new qualifications presenting today's hearing professional with nothing less than a bright future to contemplate.

But this has to be spelled out loud and clear. The world at large has to be made aware of how far hearing technology has entered the digital age and how well it competes with the games that geeks play. Young people need to be shown a career path that is less about keeping a discreet professional silence to protect personal sensitivities and much more about an upbeat confidence and pride in the latest skills and inventions that can be used to make a real difference. Hearing loss happens to all kinds of people. Connecting with them and treating them means being involved in a very special people business with many rewarding person to person contacts some of which can last a lifetime.

And what about costs? There is no denying that in 2006, the price of a top of the range hearing aid bought privately in UK and in most other European countries was high (although as we saw earlier NHS buying power could make a significant difference). Part of the pricing undoubtedly recognises the exceptional personal service that some private sector audiologists and dispensers are prepared to offer. At the same time hearing aid manufacturers would undoubtedly have been aiming to recoup their investment in research and development. However, just as with flat screens, PCs, mobiles and Mp3 players, a mass market will ultimately

Hearing for John

lead to lower price tags for hearing aids as new growth takes hold.

There are already many signs of big changes fast developing. Entrepreneurs are spotting the opportunities. Hearing aid advertisements are becoming more frequent and strident. Price cutting is the biggest single theme. Perhaps dedicated after-care will be offered as well. But how much can be given with packages bought off-the-shelf or through the internet? Time will tell.

For better or worse these activities will not only lead to more business: they will also help to increase awareness generally and give a more vibrant, exciting feeling to the whole idea of caring for hearing loss.

No longer should we allow it to hide in the shadows. Instead we *must* share it and let in the sun.

John - *Personal background*

I was 35 when my hearing loss was first identified. After four years, the exceptional loss in my right ear was diagnosed as an acoustic neuroma – a benign tumour growing on the auditory nerve. The procedure to remove the tumour unavoidably damaged the nerve, leaving me with no hearing on that side. In the following 27 years, my left ear has continued to lose hearing to the point where it now offers little more than 30% of what would be regarded as normal. Put another way, my total hearing capacity is about 15%. And yet, very fortunately, I lead an active, nearly normal life. I am only too conscious of how lucky I am.

It has been my very good fortune to receive support from highly-dedicated doctors and hearing aid audiologists, mainly in the private sector, whose advice and recommendations have led me to experience much of the best technology available at any moment in time. The cash cost for me has been high but this has been a personal choice driven by a determination to provide my deteriorating left ear with the most up-to-date hearing aids at almost any price. It was for this reason that I became officially registered as severely deaf and began to receive help from public funds only *after* digital aids were made available by the NHS – more than 25 years after my deafness was first diagnosed. This may explain why these pages do not include more comments about the work done in NHS.

In describing the steps most likely to be encountered by anyone becoming involved with partial deafness today

Hearing for John

I have pulled together my experiences with a number of hearing professionals including physicians and surgeons but, for reasons of professional etiquette, it would not be appropriate to identify them individually. The quotes that I have included under the name Professional are based on contributions from audiologists and hearing aid dispensers who have had experience in both private practice and in the NHS.

I have not chronicled the various hearing aids and treatments I have received over the years: it would serve no purpose as progress in otological skills and technology has meant many of them are no longer useful. However my not inconsiderable investment has included many of the best-known makes of hearing aid sold in UK. They took priority over other items of family expenditure including holidays.

Finally, I would like to take this opportunity to offer my heartfelt thanks to all the hearing professionals who over the years have done so much to preserve my hearing and help me to live as normally as possible. For me, their care and support have been beyond any price.

Useful Contacts

These are some of the sources of information that I have found useful.

The list is not exhaustive and I apologise if inadvertently I have omitted any important names or details.

Hearing 95 Gray's Inn Road,
Concern London WC1X 8TX

Telephone	020 7440 9871
Fax	020 7440 9872
Text phone	020 7440 9873
HelpDesk	0845 0744 600 (voice and text/local rate)
Website	hearingconcern.org.uk
e-mail	info@hearingconcern.org.uk

RNID 19 – 23 Featherstone Street,
(head London EC1Y 8SL
office)

Telephone	020 7296 8000
Fax	020 7296 8199
Text phone	020 7296 8001
Info telephone	0808 8080123
Info text phone	0808 8089000
Website	rnid.org.uk
e-mail	informationline@rnid.org.uk

Note: **'Managing Your Hearing loss: Impairment to Empowerment'** written by hearing therapists **Bunty Levene and Val Tait** is packed with valuable information and useful self-help ideas. The book can be ordered from Hearing Concern.

Deafness Research UK 330 – 332 Gray's Inn Road, London WC1X 8EE

Telephone	020 7833 1733
Fax	020 7278 0404
Text phone	020 7915 1412
Information line	0808 8082222 (free phone)
Website	deafnessresearch.org.uk
e-mail	info@deafnessresearch.org.uk

Hear-it AISBL **www.hear-it.org**
(an international information website)

The British Academy of Audiology **www.baaudiology.org.uk**

The British Society of Audiology **www.thebsa.org.uk**

The British Society of Hearing Aid Audiologists **www.bshaa.com**

The Hearing Aid Council	**www.thehearingaidcouncil.org.uk**
The UK Council on Deafness	**www.deafcouncil.org.uk**
The Eye Care Trust	**www.eye-care.org.uk**

About the Author

As producer of the BBC's first weekly television motoring programme John covered many world championship motor sporting events including Formula One Grand Prix from which he learned first-hand about the dangers to his unprotected hearing posed by extreme noise. At that time, ear defenders were comparatively rare in the pit lanes at Monaco, Monza and Le Mans, and John became aware that problems with his hearing following exposure to the roar of racing engine exhausts seemed to last progressively longer.

His partial hearing loss was positively diagnosed in his late thirties and shortly afterwards an acoustic neuroma caused a total loss of hearing in his right ear. Even so, with the help of increasingly more powerful analogue hearing aids and the skills of his hearing aid audiologists, his media activities continued to prosper. Motor sport gave way to his successful independent children's animation company where, with the help of digital hearing aids and despite further loss of hearing, he managed to maintain a 'business as usual' profile until he retired.

He now he spends his time travelling and working in UK and Spain on new creative projects. His first book, NEW & YOU, was published with AuthorHouse in August 2006.

Printed in the United Kingdom
by Lightning Source UK Ltd.
123745UK00001B/67/A